Martial Arts
and Philosophy

Popular Culture and Philosophy®
Series Editor: George A. Reisch

For full details of all Popular Culture and Philosophy® books, visit www.opencourtbooks.com.

Popular Culture and Philosophy®

Martial Arts and Philosophy

Beating and Nothingness

Edited by
GRAHAM PRIEST
and
DAMON YOUNG

OPEN COURT
Chicago and La Salle, Illinois

Volume 53 in the series, Popular Culture and Philosophy®, edited by George A. Reisch

To order books from Open Court, call toll-free 1-800-815-2280, or visit our website at www.opencourtbooks.com.

Open Court Publishing Company is a division of Carus Publishing Company.

Copyright © 2010 by Carus Publishing Company

First printing 2010

Printed and bound in the United States of America.

Library of Congress Cataloging-in-Publication Data

Martial arts and philosophy : beating and nothingness / edited by Graham Priest and Damon Young.
    p. cm. — (Popular culture and philosophy ; v. 53)
    Includes bibliographical references and index.
    ISBN 978-0-8126-9684-4 (trade paper : alk. paper)
    1. Martial arts. 2. Martial arts—Philosophy. I. Priest, Graham. II. Young, Damon.
    GV1101.M278 2010
    796.815—dc22

                                              2010027665

Contents

The Perfect Weapon
Ethics and Value

Excalibur
Western Martial Arts

Fighting Talk

DAMON YOUNG and GRAHAM PRIEST

A few years ago, we hosted a small conference at Melbourne University: 'Philosophy and the Martial Arts'. There were speakers, papers, chit-chat, and pizza—all very standard, really. But anyone walking in from the street may have been shocked or baffled. Here were a gaggle of philosophy professors, lecturers, and postgraduates, discussing how to survive a knife attack, the use of walking sticks as weapons, the pain of sword wounds, and the best way to get blood out of clothes.

By day, they lectured on logic or social justice, chatted to students and colleagues, wrote books and papers, and lamented the clogged email inbox. Their daily university routine, while not dull (well, not all the time), was quite genteel, peaceful, and cerebral.

But a few nights a week, and sometimes on weekends, many of these scholars changed. They left behind their normal gentility, and became violent. Instead of talking about truth and beauty over coffee with colleagues, they put up their fists, unsheathed their blades, or grabbed their sticks. Instead of their usual shirts and jeans, they donned strange uniforms, often stained with acrid sweat, and occasionally with blood. These polite, intelligent scholars had suffered broken arms, ribs and fingers, spinal bruising, countless bloodied noses and black eyes—and no doubt given out a few of their own. Alongside their pen driving and keyboard tapping, they'd swung fists, stabbed with swords.

Many might think it odd that a philosopher—someone committed to reason and the life of the mind—would study the fighting arts. After all, aren't intellectuals supposed to be fragile, anaemic sorts, more Martin Heidegger than headlock, more Seneca than straight-right?

As it happens, the very beginnings of philosophy, in ancient Athens, were intertwined with the martial arts. Socrates was respected as a soldier—like all citizens, he was quite literally schooled in the martial arts, the craft of battle. His courage and otherworldly calm in combat were legendary. His pupil, Plato, was a well-built grappler—'Plato', or 'broad shouldered', was his wrestling nickname. And the combative, point-for-point character of Greek philosophy had a decidedly martial mood to it.

Since then, the ties between philosophy and fighting have perhaps loosened—with the exception of Karl Marx and Friedrich Nietzsche, with their fashionable duelling scars. But the example of Socrates and Plato make it clear: martial arts and philosophy are happy bedfellows. And more importantly, they can enlighten one another. Fighting traditions and institutions are clarified by philosophical analysis, while the martial arts offer good examples of practical philosophy, or puzzles in ethics, aesthetics, and the philosophy of mind.

Most obviously, this is because many of the well-known Asian martial arts—like Karate, Kung-Fu, Judo, Aikido—were developed with philosophical ideas in mind. The Japanese martial tradition of *Budo*, for example, was influenced by the three great philosophical traditions of Shinto, Confucianism, and Zen Buddhism. As Damon Young shows in his chapter, these exist today in Japanese martial-arts schools across the world. More particularly, their customs of courtesy are associated with Shinto purity, Confucian social virtues, and the loving brutality of Zen. In his interview with Bodhidharma, Graham Priest suggests aspects of Buddhist philosophy behind Shaolin Kung-Fu—how fighting monks are seeking Buddhahood, not brawls.

But, as Scott Farrell's chapter reveals, Eastern martial arts have no monopoly on philosophical traditions. The Western tradition of chivalry, for example, can be seen as an education in, and living revival of, the ethical theories of Aristotle.

Aristotle also features in Gordon Marino's essay on the sweet science. For Marino, this exemplary Western martial art might seem uncivilised—a bloody, thuggish training in vice. But, counters Marino, it's actually an education in that classical Aristotelian virtue: courage.

Another Western martial art, fencing, also offers some intriguing philosophical questions. Nick Michaud explores the morality of

The volume editors (left, Young; right, Priest) practicing no-mind.

selfishness in fencing, while Christopher Lawrence and Jeremy Moss try to pin down what makes fencing unique and worthwhile. In other words, they use philosophy to identify the nature and value of their art. Is it the sword, the techniques, the footwork, the aristocratic aura, or something else altogether? What is the rationale at the heart of the formal duel?

Some martial arts *have* philosophies, even if they're not inspired or heavily influenced by them. That is, by training to kick, punch, choke, or throw, we sometimes imbibe certain philosophical principles. Jack Fuller argues that his training in Karate was an education in the ancient Roman philosophy of Stoicism. Travis Taylor and Sasha Cooper reveal the Utilitarian doctrines at work in Jigoro Kano's Judo. Kevin Krein argues that the martial arts are a reply to the existentialist's godless, meaningless cosmos—they provide life with order and meaning, and offer lessons in courage, discipline, responsibility, and liberty. Patricia Petersen explores the contribution of Karate to feminism: cultivating strong, independent, brave women, unoppressed by male violence or coercion. And Scott Beattie examines space in the martial arts school: how do martial artists transform their places, and how do these places transform them?

But the martial arts aren't simply *examples* of philosophy. Their ideals, customs and values are also ripe for philosophical analysis—they provide the case studies, the problems, the puzzles. Starting with the most basic, taken-for-granted part of martial arts, Bronwyn Finnigan and Koji Tanaka ask: What does it mean to act? That is, what *are* we doing when we dodge the blow of our Kendo opponent, and quickly reply with a strike to their head? Is this thought or thoughtless, planned or spontaneous? And if it's thoughtless and spontaneous, how are we responsible? Joe Lynch also uses martial arts to illuminate the nature of the psyche. In particular, he pits the Western ideas of Plato, against the Eastern ideas of the Shaolin monks. Which framework sheds more light on the fighter's mind, Plato's theory of the soul, or Buddhist ideas of selflessness and mindlessness? And Rick Schubert explores the nature of mastery in the fighting arts: is it knowledge *of* all the techniques, the training to *use* them all, the fitness to *perform* them, or something else? Just what sort of knowledge counts in the martial arts, or any craft?

Once we're masters of head-kicking or arm-locking, does this mean we're morally justified? In other words, what is the ethical nature of martial arts? Tamara Kohn explores what we owe to others in Aikido, drawing on the work of French philosopher Emmanuel Levinas. Chris Mortensen questions his own morality, that of Buddhist pacifism: can he be a man of peace *and* a martial artist? If so, just what sort of self defence is ethically justifiable? (Hint: it involves a big stick.) In different ways, Gillian Russell and John Haffner and Jason Vogel assess the ways martial arts can leave us morally compromised: ignorant, arrogant, passive or gullible. Is obedience always right? Does fighting leave us calm and peaceful, or anxious and violent? What traps await the young student with the clean white belt?

And, finally, why is this sweaty, dirty, bloody, painful pursuit so exquisitely beautiful? Put philosophically, what is the aesthetic nature and value of the martial arts? In her essay, Judy Saltzman looks into the curious charm of fighting and forms, with help from Friedrich Nietzsche.

All of these chapters are published for the first time in this volume, with the exception of Gordon Marino's, which first appeared under the title "Boxing and the Cool Halls of Academe" in *The Chronicle Review* (August 13th, 2004), and is reprinted with permission.

Not everyone will agree with every chapter—philosophy, like the martial arts, is often in conflict. But as every martial artist knows, there's nothing wrong with friendly conflict: the point is to confront it intelligently, patiently and with largeness of spirit. Sometimes, to learn the lesson, you have to wear a few bruises (if only to your intellectual pride).

Enter the Dragon

Traditional Asian Martial Arts

*"It is like a finger pointing
away to the Moon"*

1
Pleased to Beat You

DAMON YOUNG

A couple of years ago, not far from my home, a stranger grabbed me by the lapel and sleeve. I struggled, I tried to break his grip, but it was too late. He swiftly spun on the ball of his foot, whipped me over his shoulder, and dumped me onto the ground. I stiffened up in the air—a natural reflex. But it made things worse, because I hit the ground hard. It hurt. A lot. I must have looked like Sylvester

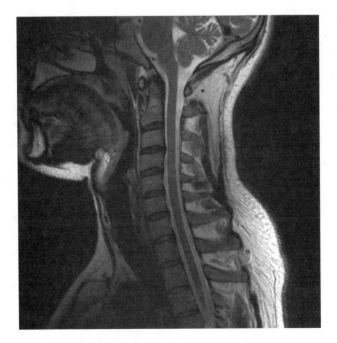

The author, proving he's not entirely spineless

the cartoon cat—I shook my head, wobbled about, and saw stars. As it turned out, I'd just damaged one of my cervical disks—a mild but potentially dangerous spinal injury.

I didn't know this. All I knew was that this bloke had hurt me, and I ached everywhere. So did I hit him? Did I hurl myself upon him, screaming Corsican oaths of vengeance? Of course not. Like any civilized practitioner of Judo, I bowed, thanked him, and moved on to the next partner. And I did the same thing when I practiced Karatedo, another Japanese martial art. Despite the bruises, the cuts, the aches and breaks, I always said "thank you"— and I almost always meant it. Courtesy was important: to me, to my teacher, and my martial comrades.

And we weren't being oddball Australians ("Sensei Bruce, meet Sensei Bruce"). The Japanese martial-arts masters often celebrated courtesy. For example, in his classic writing *Hagakure*, the samurai Tsunetomo Yamamoto (1659–1719) was at pains to stress good manners. He urged samurai to reply calmly and politely to bumbling colleagues, instead of snapping. "To treat a person harshly," he wrote, "is the way of middle-class lackeys" (Avon, 1979, p. 37). The problem seems to be that they were middle-class, not that they were lackeys.

If Yamamoto's snobbery was long-buried by the twentieth century, his ideal of courtesy was alive and well in the modern Japanese martial arts. The founder of Shotokan Karate, Gichin Funakoshi (1868–1957), thought etiquette was basic to his fighting art. "Karate begins and ends," he said simply, "with courtesy" (*Karate-Do: My Way of Life*, Kodansha International, 1984). While perhaps more prickly in the flesh, Aikido founder Morihei Ueshiba (1883–1969) saw the cosmos itself in this way. "When you bow deeply to the universe," he wrote in *The Art of Peace*, "it bows back" (Shambala, 2002, p. 92). (Having said, this, Ueshiba also told stories about dodging bullets on the battlefield.) Judo founder Jigoro Kano (1860–1922) was far more Westernized than his counterparts in Karate and Aikido, but he still thought traditional good manners and virtues were vital to his fighting art. In *Kodokan Judo*, he said that the Judo *dojo* (training hall) was not for "idle talk or frivolous behaviour," and students were to "always show sincerity" (Kodansha International, 1986, p. 33). He taught them how to break arms and choke folk unconscious—but always with fine etiquette. In the Japanese martial arts, swollen vertebrae and good manners go together.

Daniel-san: Good at Manners, Bad at Fighting

But why? Does fighting have anything at all to do with courtesy? Do we expect football hooligans to punctuate their beatings with "please" and "thank you"? Are we really hoping Mike Tyson's manners will improve? ("Dear Mr. Hollyfield, I would *so* like a mouthful of your ear.")

The short answer to each is "no." After watching *The Karate Kid*, it'd be nice to believe that well-mannered Daniel-san would really beat up the Cobra Kai louts, *because* he was polite and they were rude. It's consoling to think that virtue and etiquette are rewarded with martial supremacy; that vice and vulgarity are punished with defeat. And perhaps we take these fantasies to the arena of world politics. For example, it's nice to think that, in the great courtroom of history, Napoleon was judged and found wanting—Waterloo was the defeat of a vulgar provincial upstart, with short-man syndrome.

But this simply isn't true. Whether it was Bonaparte or Johnny the *Karate Kid* bully, their failures were of skill, not manners. They failed to use the right strategy and tactics at the right time. They might've been hampered by all sorts of character flaws—conceit, egotism, pride, and the like—but so were their enemies. At the end of the day, battles are won chiefly by a combination of luck, skill, and wherewithal. Etiquette, manners, and politeness are at best a diplomatic aid: they might stop fights, but they can't end them. "Everything," said Napoleon, "is moral in war." Or in the words of the Cobra Kai boys: "Yes, Sensei! No mercy!"

Translated into Karate or Judo, the simple point is this: if you want to be a fighter, a good leg-kick or hip-throw is worth more than a lifetime of "please" and "thank you." Whether it's politeness or civility, good character doesn't *necessarily* mean good fighting—this is a myth.

Aristotle, meet Jigoro Kano

So were Kano and his mates simply bad philosophers, or were they getting at something else? To understand courtesy in the Japanese martial arts, it's not enough to reject its masters as unintelligent, naïve, or bonkers—though when Ueshiba has a mystical vision and calls himself a "Prophet of Peace," it's hard not to be cynical. We need to look a little more closely, and a useful distinction comes from Ancient Greek philosophy: between *techne* on one hand, and *ethos* on the other.

Techne was the Greek word for "skill" or "craft", and it remains today in our words "technique" and "technology". *Ethos* meant something like a "way of life"—it's where we get our word "ethics." Aristotle (384–322 B.C.E.) gave a very helpful account of both. In his *Nicomachean Ethics*, Aristotle said that *techne* was the art of realizing possibilities. And more specifically, possibilities that wouldn't be realised otherwise. It did so reliably, and could be taught clearly by professionals to novices. Obviously, the martial arts are a classic *techne*: if medicine was the art of realizing health, the martial arts were crafts of ill-health—for enemies, at least.

But for Aristotle, *techne* was very narrow knowledge. It didn't help citizens vote, or politicians write policy. It was simply technical know-how—more at home with slaves than the free men of Athens. Any man could learn medicine or ship-building. It didn't make them free, wise, or happy.

For these, a man had to work on his *ethos*. While a *techne* was just one bit of life as a whole, his *ethos* was this life as a whole. The important thing for a good life was to cultivate character—not one part, but every part. In manner, dress, appetite, and reason, the good man had to develop excellent habits. This was why justice, for Aristotle, was the chief virtue of the good man: it had *all* the appropriate virtues in relation to others, without contradictions. So skills in medicine or ship-building had to fit in with a broader vision of life. It wasn't enough to bandage a broken toe or slap tar on a hull, and then go off and sink a ship in the harbour. Whatever *techne* was your profession or hobby, it was only ever one part of a life as a whole; and hopefully an ethical life, including courtesy.

As it happens, the Greek *techne* and *ethos* have Japanese equivalents: *jutsu* and *do*. It's not a perfect fit, but it's close enough to be illuminating. For many Japanese masters, *jutsu* were simply skills. For example, when Jigoro Kano learned *jujutsu* in the late nineteenth-century, he was acquiring *techne* in fighting, not developing his character. While some old samurai schools—the so-called *koryu* schools—did emphasise etiquette and courtesy, many later masters were quick to distance themselves from this. They were interested in what they called a "*do*," or "Way" (Chinese, "*Dao*"). For Kano, Judo wasn't simply an efficient instrument for strangling assailants or injuring the necks of arrogant philosophers—it was training in the good life. "Skill is incidental," he said in *Mind Over Muscle* (Kodansha, 2005; p. 19), using the word *jutsu*. Gichin Funakoshi also saw Karate in this way—hence the "*do*" at the end.

"Karate-do is not only the acquisition of certain defensive skills," he wrote, "but also the mastering of the art of being a good and honest member of society" (*My Way of Life*, p. 101.). In the modern era, most of the *gendai budo*, or so-called "traditional" Japanese martial arts (which are younger than Boxing), took up this philosophy. They were interested in what Aristotle called an *ethos*: whole character, not just piecemeal proficiency. Their word for this was *budo*—the "way of war."

In this light, it's not so silly to speak of courtesy and fighting in the same breath. It's not that good manners or civility *make* you a fighter, or *vice versa*. It's quite possible to be a polite weakling or a vulgar thug. The Japanese masters were saying that the craft of fighting is one part of a whole way of life; one *techne* in an *ethos*, one *jutsu* in a *do*. And more importantly, these needn't contradict one another. Courtesies can make training easier or more fruitful. Fighting can be an opportunity for practicing good manners and cultivating good character. And our pains and injuries can help us to overcome our moral shortcomings.

Yours sincerely, WHACK!

One of my keenest memories of Karate is of the moment of exquisite tranquillity before *kumite* (sparring). I adjusted my uniform, retied my belt, and tried to calm my breath. When the command "*hajime*" was given to start, I'd aim to be ready: hands up, feet steady but light, and eyes on my sparring partner. I'd try to rid my mind of pettiness, vanity, self-consciousness, and pride; to forget the worries of the day. When the fight began, my attention wasn't on homework or detention—it was on myself and my opponent; on our techniques and footwork, tentative advances, and swift withdrawals. I was trying to be single-minded, but not narrow-minded. I had a variety of techniques in my mind, but I didn't want to be conflicted or vague. When I struck, I had to be absolutely committed.

As my *sensei* explained, the Japanese word for this is *kime*. It's characterized by a spontaneous, clear, determined consciousness of oneself and another. It has an intimacy to it; a violent, brutal closeness.

In fact, it's a kind of good manners. When sparring, I didn't ignore my opponent, or try to maim him. I didn't want to exploit him for money, nor did my teacher. We were there to learn from

The author, being intimate with an old friend

one another; to give each other this violent attention, and to profit by this martial intimacy. There was a purity, not only to our perception, but also to our mindset: we were doing one another the courtesy of good, clean fighting.

In the Japanese folk religion of Shinto, purity is very important. Shinto believers have no bible or table of commandments. Theirs is a universe of millions of gods, all inhabiting the natural world. These divinities aren't lawgivers or vengeful Lords—they're all that is enchanting, awesome, and sublime in the cosmos. But they're not just *there* to be wondered at; not on the shelf in supermarket aisles ("Massive clearance on river sprites! Buy one, get a beach god free!"). Instead, the Shinto devotees have to cleanse their minds of everyday bugbears and obligations. They have to free their consciousness of contrary, inhibiting, thoughts and emotions. In simple terms, their minds have to be pure: attentive, receptive, focused.

As it happens, this purity has an equivalent in moral life: sincerity. The *Oxford English Dictionary* defines sincerity as "pure, unmixed; free from any foreign element or ingredient." To be sincere isn't just to be honest—it's to be straightforward, devoted, and single-minded. It's particularly important in the Japanese martial-arts tradition, where sincerity is sometimes more important than anything else. "Sincerity is as necessary to the human race," wrote high-ranking Judo player Sumitoro Arima, "as is oxygen to the human life; without it man can scarcely hope to live in the true sense of the word" (*Judo: Japanese Physical Culture*, Mitsumura, 1908; p. 35). For martial-arts masters like Arima, sincerity is something that pervades our whole way of life; our *ethos*, to use the Greek word.

In this light, fighting isn't *just* a skill—it reveals a state-of-mind, a way of relating to others. We not only speak and act with sincerity; we also spar with sincerity—we do our opponents the courtesy of committing ourselves, body and mind, to the fight.

Confucius Says: "Sorry about the Numb Arm, Mate"

One hot Melbourne evening, I was sparring a yellow belt in Karate. As a brown belt, I was more skilled than he was—and I was bigger, stronger, and faster. I didn't want to hurt or humiliate him, I was trying to make him comfortable and relaxed. I let my guard down so he would attack, and kept backing away, drawing him in. But to be perfectly honest, I was bored. I was exhausted from the heat of the day, the humidity of the *dojo*, and I didn't have the energy to baby-sit this beginner. Toward the end of the fight, he tried one of the techniques from our senior *kata* (forms)—a combination of block and palm-strike. Without even thinking, I quickly punched his arm out of the way, my knuckles into the nerve bundle at the side of the elbow. It was a very hard punch. He yelped and clutched his numbing arm. I felt terrible. Before my *sensei* had given the inevitable command, I was already on my knees to the side of the mat, facing the windows. I wanted to show my teacher, my opponent, and the rest of the class that I was sorry.

It's important what I *didn't* do. I didn't laugh at his pain and injury, or cry in shame. By sitting to the side in *seiza*, I was demonstrating quiet, humble regret. If I had only grazed him, or if he were a black belt, perhaps we would've kept fighting. If I'd killed him, I'd probably have cried. But this time, he just needed a little time to recover, and to know I was sorry. By putting myself in his shoes (or bare feet), I was trying to do the right thing, at the right time and place.

This idea is at the heart of Confucianism, which was imported into Japan from China. Confucianism's main text is the *Analects*, which records the conversations and sayings of Confucius (551–479 B.C.E.) and his disciples. Confucianism began in a chaotic time for the Chinese, when war, poverty and cynicism were rife. With their philosophy, they were trying to make their civilization more moral.

The most important ideal for the Confucians was responsibility. There was no simple Divine Law—if men wanted a good family and society, they had to do it themselves. The Confucians also spoke of a Way, but the buck stopped with human beings. "It is the person who is able to broaden the way," said Confucius, "not the way that broadens the person" (*Analects*, Ballantine, 1999, p. 190). Goodness comes from men, not from commandments or states.

To be truly good, the Confucian has to have *ren. Ren* is the same as the character for "man," and it's translated as human-heartedness, humaneness, goodness, benevolence, altruism, and authoritative conduct. At bottom, it's a kind of ethical generosity; a talent for doing the right thing at the right time, which helps others to do the same. The gentleman of *ren* is patient, honest and straightforward, and isn't a busybody – he's more concerned with his own character than picking on others. Put simply, he's a moral partner; a collaborator in the good life.

But to make this happen, he needs *li, yi,* and *shu. Li* means correct form, and in Confucianism this meant ritual, rite, custom. When I kneeled in *seiza* on that Melbourne evening, this was *li.* It was the form or pattern of my apology. But every form needs content—this is *yi*: the right kinds of feelings and thoughts, in the right place and time. When I hurt that yellow belt, I didn't want to show vanity, hatred or pity, just sincere regret and mild sorrow. And I might've shown different feelings in different circumstances, with a different sparring partner—there's no iron-clad rule. Confucianism is a philosophy of good character, not laws or regulations. To develop a good character, the man of *ren* has to get a knack of fitting *li* to *yi*, form to content. But to find this fit, the good Confucian needs *shu*. We might call *shu* empathy or unselfishness—"putting oneself in the other's place" (*Analects*, p. 92). This was what I was trying to do when I judged my opponent's injury, and opted for an apology. And it was the same "sorry" I would've wanted if I were hurt—not patronizing or dripping with pity, but straightforward and silent.

In this way, the point of Confucianism isn't to make people obey tyrants or toe the line (though it was used for this in China and Japan). Confucius wanted to cultivate individuals who cared for one another and their society. The idea is disarmingly simple: if we're responsible for only ourselves then we have to be careful, clear, and thoughtful. We have to know what to do and say, and when and where to do so. No book can do this for us—it just takes practice, and the willingness to learn from mistakes. When it works, it leads to something rare and precious: a community of understanding, sympathy, and trust.

By giving a place to the rituals of gratitude and regret, my Karate *dojo* was keeping this Confucian ideal alive. It was giving me the chance to use empathy, and match my feelings to the right customs and gestures; to use *shu* to fit *li* with *yi*. It was building a small community at the same time: our school. Instead of a place of mistrust and cynicism, it was a place where beginners—like my yellow belt friend—knew they could learn in safety. And crucially, we were taking these insights into our lives; witnessing about the social importance of sincerity, good manners, and trust.

In this light, my Karate school's etiquette wasn't just froth. We were being courteous so we could be properly educated: in fighting and life.

Free Your Mind, and Your Roundhouse Will Follow

Not long after I got my *shodan* (black belt), I fought in a seniors class for the first time. I was puffed up with pride, and ready to knock down all comers. I did my basics. Easy. I raced through my *kata*. No sweat. Then came the good bit: fighting.

With my crisp new black belt, I was brimming with confidence and strength. I faced my first opponent: a middle-aged man, with knocked-out teeth and a paunch. I got into my stance, put up my hands, and then waited to finish him off. It wasn't pretty. I was punched in the face, kicked in the stomach, swept to the ground and kneed in the ribs. I tried to retreat, and he followed. I tried to attack, and he defended. It was hopeless. I wanted to give up, but I wasn't even half way into the fight. And I had six or seven more matches to go. I knew they'd all be this painful and humiliating. But I kept fighting.

By the end, I was exhausted, bruised and bleeding. I wasn't thinking about the fights, or the night's pizza, or my own stinking, sweaty *gi*. In fact, I wasn't thinking about anything—I was barely there. My self-conscious, conceited, ego was gone, and I was oddly happy about it. The rest of the fights were painful and taxing, but felt natural. Even as I was elbowed in the jaw and kicked in the thigh, I felt light and absurdly free.

This wasn't the thrill of sadomasochistic play (well, not for me), but what we might call "no-mindedness." And it's often talked about in Japanese martial arts. Gichin Funakoshi spoke of the "*kara*" in Karate as the "emptiness, the void, that lies at the heart of all creation," an emptiness we must be (*My Way of Life*, p. 35). In the Australian martial-arts magazine *Blitz*, Goju-Kai Karate master Gogen Yamaguchi told interviewer John B. Will about "*muga*": "a state of nothingness . . . freed to act without interruption and thought" (Blitz, 2006; p. 58). Aikido founder Ueshiba wrote: "Return to true emptiness. Stand in the midst of the great void" (*Art of Peace*, p. 87). And long before the twentieth century, the Buddhist philosopher Takuan Soho wrote about *fudoshin*, or "immovable wisdom": a light-footed, swift-handed swordplay, which was thoughtless but unbeatable. "The mind," he wrote, "stretches throughout the entire body and self" (*The Unfettered Mind*, Kodansha, 1986; p. 32). It was everywhere and nowhere.

The philosophy behind this is Zen Buddhism. Buddhism was originally from India, and began in the sixth or fifth century before Christ. According to legend, Gautama Buddha, an Indian aristocrat, had left his family for the life of a religious ascetic. Like all Hindus, he believed that everyday life was an illusion. Senses or common-sense ideas weren't to be trusted—they were all delusions. What he sought was *Brahman*, the great One: the absolute truth beneath life's eternal changes. But sitting in meditation under the Bodhi tree, Guatama had a realisation: if all things were illusion, so was *Brahman*. To achieve salvation, the point wasn't to strip away illusions to get to *Brahman*—*Brahman* itself had to be questioned, rejected, forgotten about. And more worryingly still: if all things were false, so too was salvation.

In Zen Buddhism, this philosophy led to a unique way of life. It's captured in this poem, from Bodhidharma, a patriarch who took Buddhism to China:

> A special transmission outside the teachings,
> Not depending on the human word,
> Directly pointing to the human heart,
> Seeing into its heart, and becoming Buddha.

Instead of stressing studying, reciting prayers, and more study, it turned to humble, everyday practice: cooking, cleaning, eating—and fighting.

The idea behind this is relatively simple. For Zen Buddhists, we're not trying to become Buddha—we're Buddha already. In fact, we're not trying to become *anything*. We're simply being, without calculation, cogitation, anxiety or self-consciousness. The aim is no-mindedness: the nothingness, the emptiness of the martial-arts masters. Fine—why not just drink a bottle of Scotch? That'll empty your mind, right? "The idea is not to reduce the human mind to a moronic vacuity," wrote Alan Watts, "but to bring into play its innate and spontaneous intelligence by using it without forcing it" (*The Way of Zen*, Thames and Hudson, 1958; p. 21). But this aim is achieved by *not* aiming—by simply doing, over and over again.

There are stories of Zen masters helping their students to do this. In *Zen and Japanese Culture* (Pantheon, 1959; pp. 13–15) Daisetz Suzuki tells the story of a swordsmaster who had his student cooking, cleaning, and washing for years. When the student was busy, the master quickly thumped him with a stick. Over the years, the student slowly learned to sense the attack. One day, the teacher was cooking, and the student attacked him. The master calmly blocked his attack with a frying pan. The student suddenly grasped what he had learned, and understood the kindness of his master. What seemed like cruelty and malice was tenderness—his harsh treatment had deflated the student's ego. And in doing so, he'd learned to stop thinking, worrying, hoping, and to simply . . . do.

And this was the courtesy I enjoyed as a black belt. I was full of myself—proud, arrogant, and far too self-conscious. My seniors cured me of this. They didn't seriously hurt me, and they still bowed and thanked me for the sparring. They were sincere, conscientious, and considerate. But in their violence, they were working toward the goal of the Buddhist masters. With every bruise and cut, they were chipping away at my clumsy, over-analytic mind. This is the good manners of Zen. It's not shallow politeness, false pity, or the placation of laziness. It's the courtesy of relentless, careful brutality.

The author, foolishly trying to avoid Zen courtesy

2

An Interview with Bodhidharma

GRAHAM PRIEST

Bodhidharma was an Indian Buddhist monk, who moved to China and took up residence at the Shaolin Temple. His dates are uncertain, but his arrival at the Temple was around 500 C.E. According to legend, Bodhidharma was the first patriarch of Zen Buddhism. According to another legend, he was also the founder of Shaolin Kung Fu.

Bodhidharma, *woodblock print by Yoshitoshi, 1887,* <*http://en.wikipedia.org/wiki/Bodhidharma*>.

VOICE: And now, Radio 6UVFM, broadcasting from Xian, China, is proud to bring you a live interview from Shaolin. As you all know, there have been many reports coming from the temple there of strange goings-on. Reputed to be behind these is a new monk from India, Bodhidharma. He seems a rather elusive character, but our reporter has finally managed to catch up with him in a cave near the Temple. We take you there now.

REPORTER: Mr Bodhidharma . . .

[*Silence*]

REPORTER: Mr Bodhidharma . . .

[*Silence*]

BODHIDHARMA: Oh, sorry about that. I was just finishing this morning's meditation session. It's very hard to leave nirvana, you know.

REPORTER: Er . . . yes.

[*Pause*]

REPORTER: Mr. Bodhidharma, a lot of reports of strange events at the Shaolin Temple have been emerging recently. Apparently, groups of monks have been seen going through sequences of violent movements, and even fighting each other. That sort of thing doesn't sound very Buddhist. Some say that you are behind this. I think that our listeners would be interested to know what's going on.

BODHIDHARMA: I don't think that anything very strange is going on, but please feel free to ask.

REPORTER: Is it true that you encourage your monks to fight?

BODHIDHARMA: No . . . Yes . . . Well, . . . Yes and no.

REPORTER: Please stop being evasive. Your monks are seen to be out there fighting. Is this true?

BODHIDHARMA: Not exactly fighting—practicing to fight.

REPORTER: And you encourage this?

BODHIDHARMA: Yes.

REPORTER: Why?

BODHIDHARMA: When I arrived here, they weren't very fit. Sitting in meditation for long periods can be pretty demanding physically, and a lot of the monks really weren't up to it. So I designed a bunch of exercises that they could do to improve their fitness. The monks are now out there every morning doing them, even when it's pissing down with rain. It's hard work, but it toughens them up.

REPORTER: You could at least let them do it indoors!

BODHIDHARMA: Fresh air! Very good for breathing!

REPORTER: Well, you could just as well get the monks to go for a morning run.

BODHIDHARMA: No. It wouldn't be the same. When running, you can turn the mind off. I want the monks to be focussed on what they are doing—not thinking about what's for breakfast, or the pretty young news-reader on the TV last night.

REPORTER: Okay, but what about the fighting?

BODHIDHARMA: There's nothing like a fist hurtling within a centimeter of the nose to focus the mind!

REPORTER: You're avoiding the point. This is violence. You are teaching people techniques to hurt others.

BODHIDHARMA: Not exactly . . . The techniques can hurt others, it's true. But I'm not teaching them *to* hurt others. I don't advocate the use of aggression against others. In fact, I find that the monks who work at these techniques actually become more peaceful people. The more they practice the techniques of violence, the less violent they become—the less inclined they are to actually engage in any kind of violence . . .

REPORTER: That's odd. Usually, if you practice doing something, it makes it easier to do . . .

BODHIDHARMA: Still, I must confess, the techniques do come in handy sometimes. We live in pretty rough times. As you often report on your station, violence is on the increase. The Temple here is pretty isolated, and from time to time groups of thugs come here trying to steal. They can be pretty violent. We have to defend ourselves.

REPORTER: Is that consistent with the teachings of Buddhism?

BODHIDHARMA: Oh, yes. The Buddha taught compassion for all sentient creatures. But that doesn't mean that you have to let one of them thump you.

REPORTER: Oh . . .

[*Pause*]

Illustration from the Bubishi,
<*http://commons.wikimedia.org/wiki/File:Bubishi.svg*>

REPORTER: Can I change the subject? Is it true that you came from India?

BODHIDHARMA: Yes, I arrived a few years ago.

REPORTER: Why did you come here?

BODHIDHARMA: Well, as you know, I'm sure, Buddhism has been practiced in India for a thousand years. It's starting to catch on in China now, but according to reports coming back to India, the Chinese don't really understand Buddhism. I came here to see if I could help out.

REPORTER: What do you mean?

BODHIDHARMA: When I arrived here I found a lot of devoted monks. They were very conscientiously reading the scriptures, but they didn't really understand them. I was able to develop their understanding.

REPORTER: In what way?

BODHIDHARMA: Well, they took all that stuff so *seriously*! There's a place for that, of course, but in the end, that's not what Buddhism's all about.

REPORTER: Oh?! So what is it about?

BODHIDHARMA: You guys think that you know what reality is. But you don't.

REPORTER: What? The ever-changing world around us? I know it's described like that in the *Book of Changes* (*I Ching*).

BODHIDHARMA: The same. When you go to the shop in the morning, and buy a liter of goat's milk, you know that it won't last for ever—like everything else. Even if you don't drink it, it will change into curd.

REPORTER: Yes. So?

BODHIDHARMA: But you still think that when you make the purchase there is something, some objectively existing object, that is transferred from the shop keeper to you.

REPORTER: Isn't there??

BODHIDHARMA: No. You think there is, but that's only the way that you *conceptualize* the situation. You have this label "liter of goat's milk," and you think it applies to an object out there. But in fact it doesn't. What's out there, if I can put it a bit misleadingly, is some stuff—we give it a technical name, "tathata"; some people call it "thusness," but "'stuff'" will do—this stuff does *not* contain a liter of goat's milk, or any of the other things that you think are really out there. It's just that when we apply the name, it makes us think so.

[*Pauses*]

BODHIDHARMA: (*continues*): And for that matter, exactly the same is true of the shopkeeper and you. What's your name?

REPORTER: "Chan."

BODHIDHARMA: Well, Mr. Chan, you are no more real than the liter of goats milk. You have the illusion that you are objectively real, but you're not. All there really is, is thusness.

REPORTER: (*cockily*): Oh, so *who* is it that has this illusion?

BODHIDHARMA: No one. It's an illusion of an illusion.

REPORTER: (*doubtfully*): Er, . . . I see.

[*Ponders*]

REPORTER: So when you thump one of these marauding thugs, it's really an illusion that you are being violent to someone?

BODHIDHARMA: You could look at it like that.

REPORTER: But then their violence towards you is the same, an illusion?

BODHIDHARMA: Yes, it's the same.

REPORTER: So violence doesn't really matter?

BODHIDHARMA: I didn't say that. A violent attitude is a cause of suffering.

REPORTER: Dead right. Getting thumped isn't a very pleasant experience.

BODHIDHARMA: No. I'm not talking about the person who gets thumped. I'm talking about the person who's doing the thumping.

REPORTER: Let me get this straight. I thump you, and it's me that suffers?

BODHIDHARMA: Almost. If you have the *desire* to thump me . . . If you have this desire, it's the result of hatred, greed, or something equally unpleasant. You are suffering.

REPORTER: This *you* that doesn't really exist, right?

BODHIDHARMA: Yes, it's all part of the illusion. The illusion has to go. I said just now that you guys don't understand reality. As long as it appears that there are objects out there worth possessing, and there is a you that can possess them, then there's going to be possessiveness and so on—"attachment", as we say in the trade. This is the cause of suffering.

REPORTER: So once the illusion is stripped away, the desire to be violent also disappears?

BODHIDHARMA: Correct.

REPORTER: And you become at peace with yourself.

BODHIDHARMA: . . . and everything else.

REPORTER: Okay, so how do you do it?

BODHIDHARMA: Well, there's not much point in my telling you. Even if you believed me—which you probably don't—it wouldn't mean much to you. You must experience the illusory nature of things for yourself.

REPORTER: Myself . . . who is part of the illusion?

BODHIDHARMA: Yes, we've been though all that. Don't keep bringing it up. You have to experience thusness for yourself. Only then will you truly understand the illusory nature of this conceptual construction, which the unenlightened take for reality.

REPORTER: Ah . . . That's the point of meditation, right?

BODHIDHARMA: Right.

REPORTER: Can you tell me a bit about what meditation involves? What do you actually have to do?

BODHIDHARMA: As I said, there's no point in telling you about this. You have to do it. Why don't you come along and join us at the Temple? I think we may have a special offer on for journalists at this week.

REPORTER: Do I have to do the fighting exercises?

BODHIDHARMA: Yes.

REPORTER: In the rain?

BODHIDHARMA: Yes.

REPORTER: I'll think about it.

BODHIDHARMA: Very well.

[*He turns to go . . .*]

REPORTER: Wait. Can't you just say a *little* about what is involved in meditation? I'm sure that our listeners would be fascinated.

BODHIDHARMA: Ah . . . Fascination. Another attachment to an illusory world.

[*He hesitates, seeming to weigh up various considerations.*]

BODHIDHARMA: Very well then . . . What you have to learn to do is to see reality, thusness, without the overlying conceptual frame. You have to, as it were, learn to see through it. This isn't easy: we're so used to seeing no further than the frame. It can be done only by a process of intense mental concentration and focus.

REPORTER: So how do you do that?

BODHIDHARMA: One technique we teach beginners involves breathing. Breathing is not just getting air in and out. It is deeply connected with thusness. By focussing on it, it can act as a gateway.

REPORTER: I see.

BODHIDHARMA: No, you don't really. The understanding comes only with the practice. This is demanding work. You must work very hard, and do so again and again, till everything becomes natural. The result, when it comes, may be very sudden. But to get to this point normally takes years of practice.

REPORTER: Okay. But there's not much point in getting rid of attachments only when you are sitting meditating. You can't spend your whole life meditating. You have to get on with the necessities of life—sex, drugs, and rock'n'roll, as we say in the trade—and this is when attachment is going to be at its strongest.

BODHIDHARMA: Sitting? Who said anything about sitting? You *can* do these things sitting. That's a particularly good way for beginners. But you can do it when you are moving around too. You can meditate while you walk, for example. And, well, some physical activities which require intense mental focus and breath control are particularly conducive to this sort of mental state.

REPORTER: Huh. So you can do it while you are doing other things as well?

BODHIDHARMA: Yes, the aim in the end—though only advanced practitioners can do this—is to be able to see the world in this way *whatever* you are doing.

[*A long pause*]

REPORTER: Mr Bodidharma—

Enlightenment,
<http://en.wikipedia.org/wiki/Ens%C5%8D>.

BODHIDHARMA: Yes?

REPORTER: These martial art exercises of yours—

BODHIDHARMA: Yes?

REPORTER: They're not really about fighting, are they?

[*Silence*]

VOICE: I'm sorry. We seem to have lost the line to our reporter. We will get back to Shaolin as soon as we can. In the meantime, here is some popular Chinese music.

3
Don't Think! Just Act!

BRONWYN FINNIGAN and KOJI TANAKA

Kenzo saw a slight movement of his opponent. "Now is the time to strike!" he thought. He started moving. But before he had time to raise his *shinai* (sword) he was struck on the *men* (head) by his opponent. "Ippon!" the judge called.

Kenzo stepped back to face his opponent again. He took a deep breath. This time he would succeed in his counter-attack. He had been taught by his *sensei* (teacher) to enact the *Shinkageryu* philosophy: waiting for his opponent to make a move, then counter-striking at exactly the same time. He waited and watched his opponent. Suddenly his opponent raised his *shinai* to strike. Kenzo immediately saw his opponent was exposing his *do* (side of abdomen). "I can see an opening," he thought, "I should now counter-strike!" But before he had time to strike, his opponent struck him on the *men*. "Ippon!" the judge called.

How can Kenzo successfully enact the *Shinkageryu* philosophy of "waiting" and counter-strike at the same time? If he realises his opponent is about to move and thinks, "Now is the time!" it's too late. But if he doesn't think it's the right moment, how can he act at all? It's easy for his *sensei* to say, "You just have to do it!" The question is: how is this possible?

The Problem

Let's begin with a seemingly simple question: What is it to act? One of the most common replies is that action is 'intentional'. That is, it's not just an instinct or a reflex—like flinching at a punch, or grunting at a blow. Most philosophers accept the idea that an action is intentional if it is done for a reason. An action is intentional if, when someone asks you "Why did you do that?" you explain your action using reasons. For instance, if someone asks you "Why did you parry the opponent's *shinai* upwards?" you might answer, "Because I wanted to strike *kote* (forearm)." In giving this as a reason, you show how your action makes sense; you did a certain thing (parry upwards) so that you could achieve some other thing (strike *kote*). And, in giving this as your reason, you accept that striking *kote* is something *you* did.

Donald Davidson famously argued that this sort of explanation of action is a *causal* one (*Essays on Actions and Events*, Clarendon, 2001). That is, when you answer the question "Why did you parry the opponent's *shinai* upwards?" with the reason "Because I wanted to strike *kote*," you're revealing the *intention* that *caused* the action. Your intention is a combination of a desire for something ('I want to strike *kote*') and a belief about how to get it ('if I parry the *shinai* upwards, I will be able to expose the opponent's *kote* which will make it easy to strike it'). For Davidson, an intentional action, is caused by both a desire and belief—when combined, they are an intention.

Other philosophers have argued that there is *more* to this story. Some say that an intention that causes an action is not *just* a combination of a want and a belief. Instead, it must involve some reasoning and choice: *you* bring the want and the belief together. For example, think of all the things that you might want (to eat chocolate, to sleep all day) and then think of all the things that you believe you could do to achieve them (go to the shop, stay in bed). But simply wanting certain things, and having beliefs about achieving them, doesn't automatically make you *do* them. According to these philosophers, *you* need to bring these desires and beliefs together by *thinking* about them and forming an intention. You first think about the best thing to do, and then *choose* to do this. So, in our *Kendo* example, you must first think about and choose to parry your opponent's *shinai* upwards in order to strike the opponent's *kote* before you actually do this for your behaviour to count as an intentional action.

At this point, Takuan Soho might walk behind us and strike us with his *keisaku* (or *kyosaku*, a wooden stick). Takuan was the sixteenth-seventeenth century Zen Buddhist who provided Zen teachings to some of the sword-masters of his time, including Yagyu Munenori and Miyamoto Musashi. (See Nobuko Hirose, *Immovable*

Expedited   Expedited   Expedited

Open Books Ltd
905 W. 19th St.
Chicago, IL 60608
UNITED STATES
orders@open-books.org

Expedited

Open Books Ltd
905 W. 19th St.
Chicago, IL 60608
UNITED STATES

To: Matthew Barker
774 appleberry drive
San Rafael, CA 94903
UNITED STATES

|||||||||||||||||||||

MarketPlace: Abebooks
Order Number: 1900472
Ship Method: Expedited
Customer Name: Matthew Barker
Order Date: 2/9/2022
Marketplace Order #: 646107985
Email: barker@sonoma.edu
Marketplace Ship Method: 3 - 6 business days

Items:

Qtv Item

SKU: [illegible]

ISBN: 0812696840 - Books

SHELF 60B

Like New $2.34

Subtotal:	$2.34
Shipping:	$7.00
Total:	$9.34

Notes:

Thanks for your order!

Wisdom: The Art of Zen Strategy. The Teachings of Takuan Soho, 1993.) He would yell at us: "Don't think! Just act!" Even if you have never heard of Takuan, a command like this should be somewhat familiar to you—your teacher in *dojo* may have yelled it at you many times.

But doesn't this sound strange? As we have seen, an action is caused by an intention. And we act only because we form an intention with reasoning and choice. If there is no thinking and choosing, how can there be intention? If there is no intention, then we can't appeal to it in giving reasons for why we acted the way we did. And if we can't give reasons, we can't say the action was something *we* did (rather than it being an accident). And if we can't say that the action was something *we* did, then we can't say the action is something for which we are responsible. If Takuan's right, action, intention, cause and responsibility go out the window. Surely, this is crazy!

Yet it's not. In fact, Takuan's ideas are quite reasonable. But how, as martial artists, should we understand the message: "Don't think! Just act!"? How can our spontaneous attacks and parries be intentional actions, without involving thought at the time? To answer these questions, we need to return to Takuan.

Takuan Soho

In *dojo*, "Don't think! Just act!" is often explained in terms of *mushin* (no-mind). As any serious martial artist can testify, the word "*mushin*" can be frequently heard in *dojo*. It is *mushin* that students of martial arts (*Kendo* in any case) are told to attain. It is this idea that our *sensei*, Takuan, introduces.

In the *Fudochishinmyoroku* (the Record of Immovable Wisdom, translated as *The Unfettered Mind*, Kodansha, 1986), which is apparently a letter to Yagyu Menenori (the best known sword-master at that time), Takuan Soho addresses the question of where to *put* or *direct* our mind in the midst of our actions. "If you put your mind in the movement of your opponent's body," he writes, "your mind will be taken up by the movement of your opponent's body. If you put your mind in your opponent's sword, your mind will be taken up by that sword." And so on: wherever you "put" your mind, it's taken away from somewhere else. And at the same time, your mind stops. "When your eyes at once catch the sword of your opponent moving to strike you," he continues, "if you think of meeting the sword in just that position, your mind will stop at the sword, you lose your movements and you will be struck by your opponent." So what do we do? Takuan's suggestion is simple: Don't put your mind *anywhere*.

The mind that is not put on anything is what Takuan calls *mushin*. For Takuan, it is important to attain *mushin* in exchanging swords with an opponent. In mushin, the mind "does not stop in any place nor lack any one thing. Always let it fill up your whole 'being' like being filled with water, and it will appear in time of need."

In order to understand Takuan's teaching, we need to recognize two important points. First, Takuan tells us not to put our mind on any one thing, because there are other things we have to be aware of: the opponent's leg movement, the distance between the tip of the opponent's *shinai* and our chest, and so on. Moreover, our opponent is constantly moving and, hence, the situation is constantly changing. Being fixated on one thing means we're not alert to possible dangers or opportunities.

Second, Takuan sees thinking as a kind of trap—we're taken up with the thought, and this can slow our responses. For instance, like Kenzo we might wait for an opening in order to counter-strike. When the opponent moves, we might see an opening. Exclusively focusing on this, we might think to ourselves *"there* is an opening"

"Must . . . not . . . think . . . of . . . the . . . opening . . ."

together with the thought "I should strike there." This is reflective thinking, focusing on one thing, and consciously forming an intention to respond—Takuan thinks this stops our mind, and makes us slow. In the time we take to think, we give our opponent an opportunity to strike first.

Action and Intention

So Takuan's *mushin* is a fluid mind, focused on the entire relevant situation, rather than any particular thing. And it doesn't involve reflectively thinking about how to respond.

But doesn't this do away with intention? If our mind's directed to nothing in particular, then there's nothing in particular that we intend to do. The spontaneous blows and parries of a *Kendo* master with *mushin* start to look unintentional, or might not even count as actions at all. But can this be right? Surely *Kendo* masters intend to do what they do? Are their actions all accidents? This seems like a very strange idea.

Things aren't so strange if we remember that an action is intentional if it can be explained in terms of reasons. A master can give lots of reasons why they act the way they do. In particular, if we ask them to explain themselves, on a particular occasion, they might say something like, "That is what Yagyu would do in that situation." If you don't understand this answer, they might tell you a story like the following:

Think of the sword-master Yagyu Munenori. His skills with swords are immortalized. He is considered to be a model in swordsmanship—not because he's on posters or swap cards, but because his skills are fine enough to be replicated. Put another way, to be skilled with the sword is to replicate Yagyu: when you are a *Kendo* master, you will act as Yagyu would act.

Importantly, this offers us reasons. For any particular action, Yagyu's ways of acting are a *Kendo* master's reasons for acting. If asked to explain what they did, a *Kendo* master might answer, "I did what Yagyu would've done." In other words, the action was rational, because Yagyu would've done it. And with reason comes intention.

Training

Now, how does this help Kenzo? In trying to do the *Shinkageryu* move, "What would Yagyu do?" isn't really of any help. He wants to attain *mushin*, and respond in the way Yagyu would respond.

As usual, there is a short story and a long story that a master can tell Kenzo. The short story is: "Training!" It is through hard training that Kenzo can start acting from *mushin* and respond in the way that Yagyu would. Everyone already knows this much. What's hard is explaining what the training does, and how it does it. Unfortunately, there's no general answer—not even a *Kendo* master can give a general answer to that question. Why? Because *mushin* must be cultivated, not simply thought about or discovered like a natural law. And no well-qualified *sensei* can tell you how exactly *you* do this. You have to find out in your own way based on your body structure, temperament, style, and so on.

Still, there are a few things that a *sensei* can do to help Kenzo. For example, a good *sensei* can outline the various relevant features of the situation: the movement of the opponent, the distance between himself and the *shinai*, the position of the opponent's feet, and so on. Kenzo needs to train himself to "see" these subtleties, and their connection with responses. And he has to do this with increasing speed, so the perception and the response flow seamlessly. In other words, training fills the gap between knowledge of relevant features and appropriate responses on the one hand, and actually seeing, and responding to, all of these features at once, on the other. In other words, training allows us to "Do as Yagyu would do," without having to think about them at the time. Training combines wide, keen perception, with appropriate action—and because it is based on a model (like Yagyu), it is rational.

Intentional Action

But is this *really* rational? And can it give us genuine intention? We can see how training combines perception and response, but there's still something confusing about *mushin* here.

A *Kendo* master might give a reason, "That's what Yagyu would do," for enacting *Shinkageryu* move. Yet, when we ask a *Kendo* master *why* he did what he did, this answer doesn't seem entirely satisfactory. It looks like the master is telling us why he thinks what he did was the right thing to do in that situation. And fair enough: perhaps he parried the right blows, and landed his own. But we want to know what *reason* he had in mind when doing what he did.

Now, we know that the master didn't have any particular reason "in mind". Instead, he acted from *mushin*. How can he be rational, but not have any reasons in mind?

In fact, the master can give lots of reasons for his actions. For instance, if someone asks, "Why did you move slightly to your right as you struck the opponent's *men*?" a master might say, "Because the distance between the opponent's *shinai* and my chest slightly changed." He might also say, in response to the very same question, "Because the opponent's *shinai* moved slightly." If someone asks, about the very same response, "Why did you strike the opponent's *men*?" a master might say, "Because it was the most effective blow in this situation." A master can also refer to his understanding of the relationship between his response and the situation in refusing certain questions. If someone asks "Why did you leave your *men* exposed and vulnerable to your opponent?" he might reply, "I didn't. I was tempting him to strike my *men* so that I could counter-strike his *do*."

In providing any of these reasons for his action, the *Kendo* master is demonstrating that he accepts the action as his own. For this, it doesn't matter *what* exactly he says in giving a reason. Different answers are often required for different people or situations—you might explain a match one way to a rank novice, and another way to a competent beginner. What's important is this: giving a reason is a way of accepting responsibility for the action. Even if the *Kendo* master says, "I didn't do that, I did this," he's still affirming that what he did was intentional. He's showing you his reasons, and thereby accepting responsibility, even though he had neither "in mind" at the time.

A master might also say in reply, "Because that's one way to enact *Shinkageryu* philosophy and that's what Yagyu would do in that situation." This is the most general form of reason a *Kendo* master can give for his actions. But its generality doesn't make it simple or easy. On the contrary, his understanding of this reveals the richness of his experience and his competence in *Kendo*. He could see exactly what the situation was; could see exactly what should be done in that situation, and responded in exactly the right way. And, in fact, if this answer makes sense to you, without requiring further explanation from the *Kendo* master, this shows *your* level of accomplishment in the art of *Kendo*.

A *Koan*

So, how can Kenzo strike his opponent before being struck again? If he thought to himself "Now is the time to respond!" his opponent would strike him. If he didn't think this to himself, how could he even be acting in the situation?

If you thought that the solution to this *koan* is to provide Kenzo with a set of instructions as to *how* he can come to act without thinking, then we haven't given a satisfactory solution. In fact, there are no how-to instructions to give Kenzo. He needs to find his own way of attaining *mushin*.

What we have shown, however, is that this kind of *how* question (how can I do that?) is different from a *why* question (why did you do that?). Asking *how* Kenzo can act spontaneously, or *how* a *Kendo* master can do that, is asking about the mental processes behind this kind of action. But it is exactly consideration of mental processes that Takuan urges us to leave behind. In order to answer a how-question, we need to somehow be aware of the mental operations that made us act at the time—otherwise, how would we know in order to answer the question? But if we're paying attention to the mental operations of *mushin*, we can't act with *mushin*!

Yet we *can* answer why-questions—we just have to remind ourselves that they're not how-questions. If we are asked, "Why did you move slightly to your right as you struck your opponent's *men* (head)?" we might reply, "Because I thought that moving to the right would give me room to strike." This kind of answer seems to confuse a how-question with a why-question. It sounds like we're saying "My *thought* made me do it." And, for this to be true, some thinking needs to be in the mind. But our discussion of Takuan has revealed that this isn't the case. We can identify why we acted, without detailing how, or thinking about it at the time. In fact, we're trained to leave the thought about mental operations behind so that, eventually, we can respond without thinking.

By providing a reason, we own up to our actions and demonstrate that what we did was intentional. The reasons we give, and the reasons of others that we immediately understand, demonstrate how accomplished we are as *Kendo* practitioners. All this requires rational, intentional action. But not always reflective, calculative thought: to be a *Kendo* master is to act from a deep understanding of *Kendo*, with mindfulness of the complexity of the situation to which one is responding. And just how deep one's understanding of the art of *Kendo* is will be exemplified by what one does, and is demonstrated by one's reasons for action, and in one's comprehension of the reasons of others.

4
Plato and the Shaolin Monks Square Off

JOSEPH J. LYNCH

I was already exhausted by the physical conditioning and technique portion of my greenbelt test when I got ready for the sparring portion. All of the blackbelt instructors testing us that night had professional kickboxing experience.

Rick asked me if I was ready to go. I nodded yes, and he immediately broke my nose. My blood splattered all over his new white gi. The next few minutes were long and painful, but I passed the test—although Rick berated me for getting blood on his gi. I felt that that this was a kind of test of self-discovery of sorts. But how?

Traditional martial arts, I had always thought, are, more or less explicitly, directed at what might be called spiritual goals. You *can* train just to fight, to master an opponent, but the point of the martial arts is for you to master yourself. On one level, practitioners train to punch, kick, or throw more effectively; but on another level, punching, kicking, and throwing, as well as the rest of martial techniques, are ways in which one can know oneself. But what's the nature of this "self" that is being discovered and cultivated?

Plato's Martial Soul

To answer this question, let's turn to one of the few Western philosophers to deal with the martial arts: Plato. While most people have associated the term "martial arts" with the Asian fighting styles, there have been martial traditions in the West since Ancient times. It may be less obvious that these traditions have anything to do with a spiritual cultivation—at least not explicitly. But Plato's philosophy offers a very helpful theory of the self, and its relation to the fighting arts.

Plato developed a conception of human life based on the notion of a kind of philosopher-warrior. He was familiar with the fighting arts of the Athens of his day, as well as the prowess of the warriors of Sparta, whom he much admired. In the *Republic*, Plato presents his athlete-warrior, the philosopher-king (or queen) as having developed the ideal human soul. Sadly, Plato never put his warrior-philosopher program into practice—there are no Platonic dojos that I know of. But we do have a fairly clear account of what he takes the point of martial training to be.

Plato spends a great deal of time in the *Republic* talking about the Guardians, the athlete-warriors who would be trained to defend his model human community, and ultimately to rule it. In fact, it's pretty clear in the *Republic* that the Guardians represent the very ideal of human existence. While their physical training has an obvious practical, political, and military purpose, Plato emphasizes that the training of the body is the training of the soul. Plato's warriors must develop harmonious souls, where harshness is balanced with gentleness, and wisdom and rational ability are exhibited together with high-spiritedness and bravery.

Plato sees martial training as a battle to cultivate moral virtues. The human moral and spiritual situation is not so much understood as a battle between the soul and the body, though, as a battle *within* the soul. This has three different parts: appetite, emotion, and intellect. The important question is where, amongst these, the control should lie. Plato regarded physical education, and the conditioning associated with martial training, to be a training not just of the body but, more importantly, of the soul. And the right part has to be in control: the intellect (the rational part). He wanted to train fighters, in order that they become philosophers and rulers.

It's not surprising that how you train physically has important psychological effects. One of my own instructors would insist that we do countless knuckle pushups on asphalt, not because that provided any distinct physical advantage, but mainly to toughen us up in some way. This was more training of our minds than of our bodies. It's clear enough that military basic training, or Special Forces training, is directed not only to the physical skills of soldiers but also to their psychological dispositions. They are warriors by profession, and they need specific mental skills to do that job well. But

Plato is talking about more than these fairly obvious connections between psychological and physiological fitness.

For him, the athlete-warrior represents the *essence* of what it is to be human. Plato thought that since having a rational soul defines us as human beings, the person with the just and rational soul is the most fully human. The philosopher king (or queen) epitomizes this human ideal. And while we might expect Plato to offer a human ideal that is more like an ivory-tower academic, instead, the model is one where philosophical reflection is tempered by physical conflict. Indeed, the ideal person-soul is characterized by not only bravery, but also gentleness. The ideal human being has a harmonious soul, providing a delicate balance between aggressiveness and

reflectiveness. The ideal for warriors and for human beings generally is to balance aggressive tendencies with philosophical reflection.

One young man from a dojo at which I trained was particularly gifted physically, and took his new-found martial knowledge to the streets. His disposition to brutalize others earned him a severe punishment at the dojo and he was ultimately banned. From Plato's perspective, he was not developing the rational component of his soul, and thus failed to control his aggressive tendencies. True martial progress requires both reason and spirit, and most importantly, rational self-control.

Bravery

Plato's view can be illustrated well by considering the example of bravery. The ideal human life will naturally exhibit certain virtues. And virtues are rightly understood in terms of function. For example, sharpness is a virtue of a sword, since a sword's function is cutting. A sharp sword will cut well.

Plato, like other Greek thinkers, held that there are certain *moral* virtues that characterize what it is to live a good human life; in particular, wisdom, bravery, moderation, and justice. A warrior especially must exhibit bravery. This makes sense to anyone who has fought as a soldier, or indeed stepped onto the mat, ring, or cage for martial competition. The prospect of death or even serious pain can be quite daunting indeed.

To the Greeks of Plato's time, bravery meant just standing by your post. The fighter does not flee. And while we can understand this—obviously fleeing would appear to indicate cowardice, the very opposite of bravery—there still seems to be something wrong with this particularly conception of bravery. After all, you could stand by your post, simply because you did not grasp what dangers might befall you. If you don't know you're about to die, it's unlikely you'll run away!

Plato's remedy was to include an intellectual dimension to the concept of bravery. In the *Republic*, he defines bravery as "remembering what ought and ought not to be feared." Bravery is not the *absence* of fear; instead reason, as it were, puts fear in its place. After all, any martial artist, no matter how well trained, could face a situation in which staying to fight means getting a beating, and possibly even dying. It's not necessarily fear if one runs away. Bravery has a clear *rational* component.

When I tested for my black belt in Honolulu, after engaging in full-contact sparring for what seemed to me to be an eternity, I turned to face yet another opponent. This opponent was much younger and larger than I, and was already a successful veteran and later champion in his weight class of the UFC (Ultimate Fighting Championship). I certainly experienced fear at first, but then I understood that I didn't need to fear this situation.

To be sure, Plato's fighters have physical skills. Martial training does give us various physical skills. And as a practical matter these include the skills of self defense (as well as the defense of the whole community). Plato often compares his athlete-warriors to animals that are bred and trained to fight. But the difference, for Plato, is that the athlete-warriors rule themselves—they are fighters to be sure, but they have trained their souls to be ideally rational, and thus to epitomize the essence of what it is to be human. And what it is to be human is to have a well trained rational soul. To fall from this ideal amounts to a kind of dehumanizing degradation. Thus, Plato's model martial artist represents the human ideal, the embodiment of reason.

Mind and Body

There's more to things than this. Plato views the soul as quite literally imprisoned by the body. Part of the reason that Plato's Guardians can be brave is that they have identified themselves not with their bodies but with their souls. Indeed in another of Plato's works, the *Phaedo*, he says that ultimate goal of philosophical training is to free oneself from the body. Philosophical martial training may be useful insofar as one has the misfortune of remaining an embodied being. The practical aspect of martial training is primarily, if not exclusively, bound up in the practical politics of mundane existence. However, the ultimate goal is the soul's disembodiment through direct knowledge of the higher things. (For Plato, these are abstract forms; but we needn't go in to that.) So, while martial training seems important insofar as Plato has represented an ideal human life in the context of his ideal society, in the end, it will be given away when it has served it function.

This is because Plato, at heart, believes there is a noble and good essence of humanity. This soul, the true self, is a kind of a substance, a thing; and it's a thing with an essentially rational character—while the body is a kind of unfortunate impediment to full human development. And Platonic martial and philosophical practice aims at the cultivation, harmonizing, and purification of this self.

So, is this all? Have we solved the problem of the fighter's "self"?

Bodhidharma

Not really. Like many martial artists, my experience of martial arts is more "Eastern" in character. I first got interested in the martial arts watching the TV show *Kung Fu*. I was intrigued by the idea of the Shaolin monk, a peaceful Buddhist monk and skilled fighter. For others, it was Bruce Lee, or other Asian masters. Common to many of these experience is the centrality of Buddhist philosophy—which is quite at odds with Plato's.

While many of the stories about these Buddhist warriors are no doubt legends, there was for many centuries, and still is, a Buddhist martial arts tradition in Shaolin and elsewhere in China. And the various martial arts of East Asia have, to some degree at least, embodied a kind of Buddhist conception of the nature of the self, mixed with some helpful ideas from Chinese Daoism as well. The martial practices themselves may be rightly viewed as practices aimed at achieving a conscious realization of this particular conception.

All these things were retained in the martial arts of other Asian nations, adding in other indigenous idea. The *do* of Judo, Kendo, and other martial arts, were regarded primarily as paths of spiritual cultivation. The very idea of the *do* in Budo is the concept of *way* or *path*; it is the Japanese transliteration of the Chinese *Dao*. The Asian martial arts are a philosophical practice with primarily (though not exclusively) Buddhist theoretical aims. The Japanese and other Asian martial arts have their own distinctive histories, but Buddhist conceptions run through them all.

Buddhism has a quite different conception of the self—or better, of the no-self; and Buddhist martial practice aims at the direct realization of this no-self rather differently. Let's see how.

The Buddha, who, by the way, was a member of the warrior caste prior to becoming enlightened, held that there were three marks of existence: suffering (or unsatisfactoriness), impermanence, and no-self. The rough idea is this. The human condition is unsatisfactory, because everything and every experience is impermanent. We crave something permanent, even eternal, but nothing in our experience measures up. There is nothing of substance in our experience, including our own selves. There is no substance-self at all, but we cling to the idea that there is. Our craving for permanence and clinging to selfhood are what causes the human condition to be unsatisfactory. The Buddha's remedy was that once we recognize impermanence and no-self, we can abandon our clinging and craving, and thus find peace.

No-Self

But if there is no self, what is a person? Buddhism understands a human being as a psycho-physical unity. A person is conceived of as composed of five "aggregates", or the five heaps, or five streams. I think it's best to think of the aggregates as five processes, one physical, and the rest mental.

The first of the five aggregates is simply the body, its form, and the physical energies required to sustain it. The second is feeling: pleasure, pain, and neutrality. The third aggregate is perception or conception, whereby we make sense of our experience. I see an image, and then recognize it as a human being or tree. The fourth aggregate is volition, willing, thinking, imagining. And the fifth aggregate is consciousness. This notion of consciousness is not to be identified with a "self" but rather is simply various kinds of awarenesses we have by which we take in raw experiences (tongue consciousness, nose consciousness, eye consciousness, ear consciousness, body consciousness, and mind consciousness—the six sense fields). These five aggregates form what it is to be a person.

And the aggregates themselves are always changing as well. There is no substantial self or permanent person. There is no soul. There is no self of substance that possesses these aggregates. It's not even right to think of the self as identical to the aggregates. A person is more like a process or a series of functionally interrelated events.

One famous Buddhist analogy compares a person to a chariot. The chariot is not identical to any of its parts; when one looks for the essence of the chariot, one finds none. The chariot exists as a functional interrelationship of its parts. There is no chariot beyond that.

Training the No-Mind

For Plato, you train the body in order to train your soul. But from the Buddhist perspective of the Shaolin monks, there is, strictly speaking, no "self" or soul to train. Maybe it would be more accurate to say that there is no *permanent* self. None of the aggregates that comprise the self is permanent; we are constantly in flux. And the quest to seek a permanent self will naturally promote frustration if there is, in fact, no permanent self to be found. Liberation (nirvana) is to be found in the complete experiential awareness of this situation, and experience of this no-self.

In the early days of Buddhist practice, various meditation techniques were taught that could ultimately lead one to the direct experience of no-self. From the perspective of a Shaolin warrior-monk, this is also the point of martial training.

Okay. So the Buddha thought that the false view of a permanent self leads to selfishness and egoism. One clings to one's own interests, disregarding those of others, increasing suffering for all. In awakening, the Buddha is said to have realized that the awareness of the absence of self promotes selfless loving kindness and compassion for others. But we are talking about the fighting arts here. Aren't martial arts the skills people learn to beat other people up? Does it even make sense to speak of selflessly punching, kicking, or throwing your opponent?

Martial arts stars like Bruce Lee thought so. He famously advocated that no-self was at the very core of martial training, that it that blurred the line between fighter and opponent—they're both a part of the same dance. Still, it appears more than paradoxical to claim the fighting arts are really about generating selfless compassion. But that is ultimately what the arts are for—or at least *should* be for.

From Mindfulness to No-Mind

The concept of *mushin* (no-mind) is familiar to many who study martial arts. One learns to flow with the situation and achieve a fluid spontaneity. The martial artist appears to act as an agent, but a felt sense of agency has disappeared. No longer is there a distinction between yourself as a subject and your opponent as an object.

You can think of *mushin* as the direct experience, or at least a taste, of no-self. Of course, experiences might be misleading. Maybe the Platonic substantive conception of the soul is right anyway. A substantive self is not strictly inconsistent with the experience of *mushin*. Nevertheless, Plato doesn't advocate anything like *mushin*, and the Buddhist conception of no-self as an experiential possibility and goal does seem to explain these sorts of experiences in the practice of meditation and the martial arts. Most who have experienced the spontaneity of *mushin*, describe it as liberating, which makes a lot of sense from a Buddhist perspective.

Martial Practice

According to this conception of things, martial practice is a physical practice that seeks to transform us both physically and psychologically to no-self realization. From the Buddhist perspective, the false conception of a substantial enduring self is a prime source of suffering, *dukkha*, to be ill at ease, to be not at peace. The realization of *mushin* is the direct experiential realization of no-self, which can eliminate this impediment to being a person of peace.

This sounds like a surprising claim. Martial arts, after all, are fighting arts. And it might be just as likely that the martial artist who experiences *mushin* would have no qualms about behaving violently. There's nothing intrinsic to the physical practice of the arts themselves to exclude this possibility. Thus, it might seem that a realization of no-self or no-mind could be nihilistic or otherwise have disastrous results. Perhaps *mushin* and no-self frees one from moral responsibility. The martial artist can really harm others effectively and without remorse.

Followers of Plato might argue that this is why human beings need the constraint of reason. Might this show that a Platonic or similar conception of the rational self is more adequate than the Buddhist conception? The problem here is reminiscent of the dispute between Daoists and Confucians. Daoism takes Confucian talk of virtue to be antithetical to the spontaneous natural way of the Dao. The Buddhist perspective of the Shaolin monks certainly does recognize the importance of an ethical life. But I think that the Buddhist idea that is exemplified in martial training is that the experience of no-self allows for virtuous behavior to arise naturally and spontaneously from one's inner being.

And the Winner Is . . .

We've seen that the moral and physical spontaneity which characterizes the essence of martial training can be based on a metaphysical notion that is central to Buddhism. While the practices of throwing, kicking, punching, wielding swords, and the like may seem to be an odd way to realize no-self, they are perhaps no more odd then the practice of sitting in meditation, a practice the Buddha himself advocated, as do many martial practitioners.

The point of sitting is, in part at least, to develop the discipline of mindfulness. And you can be mindful in sitting, walking, or practicing martial arts. It's a mindfulness that leads to the realization, paradoxically, of no-mind, which is the experience of no-self. Form training is like this. One moves deliberately, sometimes quite slowly, in ways that have clear martial intent. But consistent training in this way results, ultimately, in martial virtue, the ability to move mindlessly, effortlessly, in appropriate responses to whatever situation one finds oneself in. The mind-body is trained and ultimately no-mind, no-self, is realized.

So, who wins? It's not clear that the process, no-self, view of the Shaolin Buddhist fighting monks is intrinsically more plausible than the substantive view of a rational soul advocated by Plato. On the theoretical level, this is going to be a close call. (I haven't even spoken of the matter of personal identity: what it is for a person to be the same person over time. That's enough to keep Plato and the Shaolin monks fighting for a long time!) But on the practical level, especially as related to the practice of the martial arts, I'd have to give the decision to the Buddhist fighting monks.

The Buddhist conception of no-self, together with some Daoist ideas, helps understand our martial practice. Martial arts are a way of putting no-self theory into practice in a very direct way. A problem is that such philosophical and moral underpinnings are, at best, only implicit in the actual practice of martial arts. This is unfortunate. Martial practice can be reduced to mere sport or play, but can also degenerate into egoism and "might is right." The opportunity is there, nonetheless, for the martial arts to provide a unique context for becoming fully human. At least Plato and the Shaolin monks can agree on that.

5

Now Who's the Master?

RICHARD SCHUBERT

From Miyamoto Musashi of the Niten Ichiryu to Morehei Ueshiba of Aikido, from blind Master Po of *Kung Fu* to Mr. Miyagi of *The Karate Kid*, there's no figure in the martial arts more intriguing than that of the master. Central to the martial arts from the standpoint of tradition and popular culture alike, the master is commonplace in both fictional treatments of the martial arts and real-life martial arts training. Despite this, it's hard to find an account of martial mastery that's more than superficial.

After I had trained Hapkido for twenty-five years and been tested many times, my master handed me a certificate with great ceremony and congratulated me on becoming a master myself. But what is it I had become? Many people seem to think that a master must be a maximally advanced martial arts practitioner possessed

of secret technique, who can perform all sorts of mind-blowingly difficult martial arts movements flawlessly. I don't think so.

Masters versus Masters

"Master" is used in many ways. There's the polite use. Some martial arts students address their instructors (and other people's) as "Master," intending nothing more than a show of respect. Then there's the use of "master" to express a relationship, as in the phrase "my master," which some martial artists employ to refer to their teachers, honoring the special relationship between them (whether or not their teacher is a master in a deeper sense).

There's also the use of "Master" as a formal title, used to communicate that a person holds a very advanced rank. Black belts are worn in many styles, to signify *dan* (or "degree") ranking, usually attained only after a slew of training. "Master" signifies a fourth or fifth *dan*, or higher. You can't be too exact about the specific rank of masters, since conventions vary across martial arts. Korean styles like Hapkido and Taekwondo tend to award the title "master" at fourth *dan*; Japanese styles like Aikido and Karate often award the title only at fifth *dan*.

But titles and even rank are only as good as the level of attainment those who hold them have achieved. The use of "master" as an evaluation (formal titles aside) conveys that someone has (or is believed to have) reached a very advanced level in a martial art. But what can we say that's more specific than that?

Round One: Secret Strike

One of the few detailed accounts of mastery I've ever come across claims that mastery is about secrets (Forrest Morgan, *Living the Martial Way*, Barricade Books, 1992). According to this "Secret Knowledge Account," what makes *Crouching Tiger, Hidden Dragon*'s Li Mu Bai a Wu Dan master is that he's learned not only the ordinary techniques of Wu Dan but also "the secrets of Wu Dan's highest martial arts." (Of course, he's too humble to claim having done any such thing, preferring to assert that "like most things" he is "nothing.")

The Secret Knowledge Account hinges upon the distinction (perhaps most clearly discernible in traditional Japanese martial arts) between the traditions of a school at large and its *okuden* or "hidden teachings," what others have called the *"hiden"* ("secret traditions") or *okugi* ("inner mysteries") of a martial system. To come back to *Crouching Tiger*, evil Jade Fox's illiteracy kept her from doing more than merely studying the diagrams of the Wu Dan secret manual which she stole from Li Mu Bai's master before she poisoned him. But even if she'd been able to read, she couldn't have fully understand the manual without the help of a master.

In earlier times, some techniques were military secrets. Use of these techniques, unfamiliar to the opponent, could determine the outcome of a battle. Access to such techniques was restricted to preserve secrecy and hence effectiveness. This restriction of access created a distinction between masters and other practitioners of a martial art. On the Secret Knowledge Account, mastery requires learning *both* the traditions of a school at large *and* its "hidden teachings."

Unfortunately, whatever historical merits it might have, the Secret Knowledge Account can't be a correct account of mastery in the martial arts. There are masters in the present day; but, the Buddha Palm of *Kung Fu Hustle* aside, martial arts these days don't have hidden teachings. You might (unlike me) think this means that no one is really a martial arts master anymore. More likely, you might think the Secret Knowledge account is wrong, but some other account that still agrees with what it's getting at is right. Let's call this the "the Complete Knowledge Account."

Round Two: Schubert Counters

According to the Complete Knowledge Account, what's right about the Secret Knowledge Account is that it makes knowledge of a *whole* system a requirement of mastery. Someone's a master only if they have "learned an entire system," a style's entire collection of techniques, patterns, principles, and strategies.

The trouble with the Complete Knowledge Account is that it seems to confuse attaining mastery with holding what traditional Japanese arts call the *mokuroku* or "full license"—which some martial-arts teachers used to issue, to indicate that "the teacher had taught his pupil all he knew" (R.P. Dore, *City Life in Japan: A Study of a Tokyo Ward*, University of California Press, 1967). Let's see why.

A martial art can survive changes in its catalog of techniques. The very same martial art might at one time lack a technique that it later came to include, or come to drop a technique that it once

included. Studying with the founder of a style or senior disciple of a system can mean navigating a shifting set of techniques. So, it's a mistake to tie mastery to a fixed set of techniques.

Years after my master congratulated me on achieving mastery in my own right, he decided to add to the pre-black-belt curriculum of our system of Hapkido a new takedown I'd never even seen before. I had little difficulty learning it, but I did have to learn it. Was my mastery temporarily subverted or suspended by the addition of this technique to the system? According to the Complete Knowledge Account, it was. I don't think so.

The Complete Knowledge Account gets other cases wrong as well. For many years I trained with a highly accomplished but sometimes forgetful master of Iaido, a highly detail-oriented forms-based sword art. After I had already practiced a set of forms under his tutelage for a number of years, he happened upon a set of notes he had once taken while studying with his own master, only to discover that he had inadvertently altered one part of one of the several dozen forms in the style, leaving out a step and substituting another from a different form. Was he bereft of mastery until his notes jogged his memory? Was the attainment of his most advanced students merely illusory until that day? The Complete Knowledge Account says that he was, and they were. I don't think so.

Still, there's *something* right about the Complete Knowledge Account's suggestion that a person is a master of a system only if they have learned the entirety of that system. Someone can't be a master of a system if they haven't learned the *essential* techniques, patterns, principles, and strategies of that system (including those which are, or have historically been, *okugi*).

Some things are essential to a particular martial art, and some things are merely "accidental" features. It's essential to the Drunken Style (at least *à la* Jackie Chan's original *Drunken Master*) that its techniques can be performed only by the intoxicated; no drinking, no drunken style. But it's just an accident that Su Hua Chi drinks *sake* in particular. In *The Legend of the Drunken Master*, Won Fei Hung drinks industrial alcohol rather than *sake* to perform the Drunken Style. The Complete Knowledge Account treats every element of a system as though it were essential. That's going too far.

There's an illuminating parallel between mastery of a martial art and fluency in a language. Fluency in a language doesn't require that you have learned the *entire* language, every word, for example. There are fluent speakers of English who haven't learned the word "pasigraphy." (I'm one of them! Don't ask me what it means.) But fluency does require that you have learned a certain core vocabulary. A person is not fluent in English if they haven't learned the word "is" or "the." Similarly, a person has not mastered Shotokan Karate if they haven't learned a front kick, whatever else they may have learned.

Fluency in a language also requires learning representatives (perhaps even essential representatives) of particular grammatical *sorts* of words, for example, adjectives and nouns. Similarly, mastery of a martial art requires learning representatives (perhaps even essential representatives) of essential *kinds* of techniques. Thus, for example, a person isn't a master of Taekwondo if they haven't learned jump-spin kicks, and a person isn't a master of Hapkido if they haven't learned to throw using joint manipulations.

Perhaps, you will think, I have fallen prey to "the tradesman's perspective," confusing the notion of mastery in the context of martial arts with that of mastery in the context of a trade, like sheet-metal working or carpentry (see *Living the Martial Way*, pp. 289–290). Carpenters who take classes, complete apprenticeships, and then work for a number of years, are eligible to take a trade-union sanctioned test. If they pass the test, they're master carpenters. But they don't have to know everything about carpentry to pass the test; they just have to have learned the essential techniques of carpentry. Martial-arts masters, on the other hand, must have learned more than just the essentials of their styles; they must have learned an entire system. Their knowledge must be complete.

I disagree. Mastery in the martial arts is, in fact—traditionally, at any rate—very much the same as mastery of other arts or, as we would now say, trades (Oscar Ratti and Adele Westbrook, *Secrets of the Samurai*, Castle Books, pp. 165–68). Swordsmiths in Japan were not martial artists as such, but they traditionally went through studies parallel to those of martial artists, and attained parallel understanding. Moreover, no self-respecting martial-arts master would ever takes themselves to "know it all." Morihei Ueshiba, for example, famously reported himself to be discovering new things about even elementary Aikido techniques long after the point at which he was clearly a master. He thought he still had a lot to learn from his daily practice. Mastery is quite an achievement, but even masters still have room to grow further.

Knowledge and Mastery

So far, I've been a bit vague in talking of a master's knowledge. I've merely mentioned what a master has "learned." Let's be more exact.

Philosophers often distinguish between "knowing that," "knowing how," and "having the physical ability to do" (see David Carry's

"Knowledge in Practice," *American Philosophical Quarterly*, 1981). Some examples will make the point clear. Every martial arts movie buff knows *that a spearhand is a strike with the fingertips.* That's *knowing that.* But only those who've received instruction know how to actually throw a spearhand. That's *knowing how.* It's one thing to be able to talk about something; it's another to really understand it.

The distinction between "knowing how" and "having the physical ability to do" is, perhaps, not quite so obvious. Well before I became a first *dan* I knew how to jump-spin heel-kick. I'd even used the technique to break several boards at a time on a number of occasions before I became second *dan.* While a second dan, however, I broke my foot in a half dozen places free sparring. The day my foot came out of the cast I had been wearing for the six weeks it took my bones to heal, I didn't have the physical ability to throw a jump-spin heel. In fact, I didn't even have the physical ability to walk. Still, I *knew how* to jump-spin heel—and I knew how to walk. What was impaired was my physical ability. So you can know how to perform a technique while lacking the physical ability to perform it.

Conversely, you can have a physical ability to do a technique without knowing how to do it. The first time I ever swept someone off his feet sparring, I had no idea what I'd even done; it was entirely accidental. But it was still, clearly, a demonstration of a physical ability (even if a physical ability I wouldn't really understand or learn how to employ at will until years later). In fact, the physical ability to neutralize a blow doesn't require knowledge of any kind; a Wing-Chun wooden dummy can do it, but clearly knows absolutely nothing.

I think mastery essentially involves both *knowing that* and *knowing how,* but that it doesn't essentially involve the *physical ability to do.* This might strike you as misguided. Surely a master must be able to perform mind-blowingly difficult martial arts movements! I don't think so. The temptation to think otherwise involves one of two mistakes.

The first consists in confusing a contingent (accidental) feature of mastery with an essential one. Mastery involves the physical ability to do, in so far as the physical ability to do happens to be involved in the process of coming to *know that* and *know how.* So mastery relates to the physical ability to do, in the same way that it relates to experience. Some people think it's necessary for someone to be a master that they have a certain wealth of martial experience. But it seems to me that this confuses mastery with the secondary (and accidental) result of the process which, under favorable circumstances, eventuates in mastery.

The second is the mistake of confusing what something is with how we recognize when it's present. We ordinarily *recognize* masters to be masters because of what we see them do. But that doesn't make the ability to do essential to mastery. We ordinarily recognize *dan*-ranked martial artists by the black belts they wear, but they'd still be *dan*-ranked without the article of clothing. I assure you my Hapkido master is just as martially accomplished wearing his street clothes!

Some people think holding a certain rank is essential to mastery. The usual suggestion is that a person is a master of a system only if they hold the highest technique-based (as opposed to organizational) rank in their style. But this confuses the title of master with mastery in the deeper sense that depends only on real martial attainment.

Mastery in this deeper sense is about a level of understanding. Rank is about getting promoted. System politics or geographical barriers can keep someone from being promoted to fourth or fifth *dan* regardless of their advanced understanding. After I'd studied with him a number of years, my Iaido master, a bit of an iconoclast, once offered me the opportunity to test for *dan* ranking in Iaido before the soon-retiring grandmaster of the system. The only hitch was that the test would take place several thousand miles away later that same month. Unable to reconfigure my schedule, and unable to afford the flight, I passed up the opportunity. During the next several years, I continued my formal study of Iaido; testing was never mentioned again. To this day I hold no rank in Iaido. Doubtless, some whose attainment is far greater than mine can offer similar stories.

On other occasions, I've observed individuals receive promotions just because it was politically expedient for the organization to which the person belonged to have them promoted. In one case, for example, I observed someone promoted because it "looked bad" to have them in a key position when they weren't yet a fourth or fifth *dan*, and there was no one else who already had that rank available for the post. Promotion to some relevant rank is, at best, a *sign* of real attainment, not to be confused with the thing signified.

Now, as I have said, it does seem to me that mastery involves physical ability to do in so far as this is related to *knowing that* and *knowing how*. And these are normally related, other things equal. Under ordinary conditions, the *knowing that* and *knowing how* essential to mastery are manifest in physical ability (and rank). My point is merely that they need not be. A master beset by the infirmities of old age is still a master, as is a master in a full body cast. The master in Jet Li's *Fist of Legend* looses all his fighting abilities and then his life as a result of poisoning, but dies a master just the same. To come back to the analogy with fluency, a person fluent in English who has just had extensive oral surgery or who has had a stroke affecting only their motor skills isn't able to speak a word of English, but remains fluent just the same. This isn't to deny that under ordinary conditions fluency is manifest in a person's speech.

So you could sum up what I've been saying in this way: a person is a master of a martial art just if they have thorough *knowledge that* and *knowledge how* of a set of techniques, strategies, and principles of which that martial art *could* have entirely consisted. There's much more to be said about the ideas of *knowing how* and *knowing that* which I've been using. And there is much more to be said about the similarities and differences between the application of those ideas in the context of the martial arts and in the context of crafts, performing arts, and language. There's also much more to be said about the relationship between mastery of a style or system (with which I've concerned myself here) and mastery in a sense transferable to any activity. The legendary Musashi, for example, claimed that once he had mastered his martial way, he had no further need of another teacher in martial arts, Zen, painting or sculpture (*Book of Five Rings*, Bantam, 1982; p. 6). It stands to reason that it isn't easy to master mastery.

The Karate Kid

Character and Education

*"You remember lesson about
balance? Lesson not just
karate only. Lesson for whole
life. Whole life have
balance, everything be better.
Understand?"*

6

An Enemy Lying in Ambush

JACK FULLER

Trying to hold a *shiko dachi* stance for ten minutes was too much for me. I fell over. A number of sensei with black belts looked at me. Friends looked at me. The gods of every teenage nightmare—shame, weakness, failure—sent down scribes to record the event for future use in teenage dreams and humiliating playground events.

One of the parents cracked open a can of coke. Otherwise: silence. The twenty other karateka remained in line, holding *shiko dochi*. I arose, thought of my uncle—a marathon runner—who once told me "It's just a matter of breaking the pain barrier." I rejoined the line, legs aching, and fell over again, thus ending my first attempt at Eighth Kyu grading. Much as I liked my white belt, I felt as though this was not the most graceful way to keep hold of it.

True to the art, I practiced Karate the way I practiced life. As though the gods were guiding me, I rarely missed an opportunity to fail embarrassingly in front of my friends. I joined the cricket team, the athletics team, the soccer team, and tripped or got tangled up in my own legs with the ease of a daddy-long-legs spider trying to do two *kata* at once. At fourteen years old, I understood this to be my Fate, my *Do*. It was written. I was to follow the path of the unco-ordinated and not particularly muscular. But my sensei had planted a seed. She had told me that, although I was very flexible, I needed some self-control. (At the time, I was sitting on the dojo floor attempting to hold my foot behind my head as my own warm-up exercise.) During *kata* she used to say that "discipline is the first step to defeating enemies."

Do actually means "way" not "fate". Karatedo—"way of the empty hand"—taught me my first lesson in grace and redemption:

that although one might be born as flabby as Winston Churchill, then stretched out to resemble a beanstalk, co-ordinated action can arise from the mind. If you can discipline your body, it will follow. The body needs the mind's control; the mind needs the body's action. Karate is this training. Karatedo means to situate that action within a life. How do these two relate—life and Karate training? Can we translate one into the other? In the dojo, it's pretty obvious how to use discipline: it's given by the *kata* or the rules of *kumite*. But outside the dojo, does this apply to more than self-defence? How do we use discipline in life?

Discipline on the Veranda

Two thousand years ago, a philosophy arose in Greece to consider exactly this question. The answer it gave was surprising: a truly free life requires intense discipline; a lack of discipline, one way or another, leads to servitude. This philosophy was actually used to train teenagers, to stop them being childish and turn them into admirable citizens. But it spread much further than this. These teenagers became Roman emperors and politicians. The philosophy gave rise to Christianity (along with other influences), it underpinned the British Empire, and has been read and used by the American military, in the way that Eastern martial arts (*bujutsu*) inform modern militaries (*defendu*). The philosophy started as a conversation on a veranda (*stoa*) in ancient Athens. It came to be known a "veranda philosophy" or *Stoicism*.

There were no barbecues in ancient Athens, but if there were, the Stoics would have had one there. If it had happened today, the conversation would probably have started at a lawn bowls club on a sunny day, over a beer with some mates and some neighboring bowlers. The Stoics were keen to make their philosophy a public one: it had to be useful to people in everyday life. Their approach was also more ambitious than just a cheap technique: they wanted to define a way of living, a satisfying way of growing up. Philosophy, for them, was not just something to talk about. The best indicator of someone's philosophy, they said, is not what they say but how they behave.

Karatedo is not practiced for its own sake. Similarly, Stoicism was not academic. On the veranda the Stoics wrote a training manual: for using discipline in life. You can still buy the manual today. It's by Epictetus, and called the *Enchiridion* (Dent, 1955). It was actually written down many years later as a summary of the teachings—"for the busy man." The German emperor Frederick the Great would never go campaigning without this book.

Lesson one: that the highest goods are virtues of behavior: prudence or wisdom, courage, moderation, and justice. These are things under our control. Power, money, fame, and emotions are tools, to be employed in developing these higher virtues. This is not because money is unimportant, but because money and power must be put to some use. Epictetus's curriculum was not about "revenues or income, or peace or war—but about happiness and unhappiness, success and failure, slavery and freedom." Better to be virtuous (you can be rich or poor) than to lead a bankrupt and capricious life, which money or power cannot remedy.

Lesson two: if you are a Stoic, you always keeps two separate files in your mind. One file, for things that are "up to you," or within your control, and the other file, for things that are "not up to you." The things beyond your control cause fear and anxiety. The things within your control are the proper subjects for your total focus and involvement. In Karate, this difference is held within the concept of *Do,* or "way." Choosing a particular way is not the same as accepting fate—rather, a "way" involves the external context, plus your own mind and will. The Stoics found it very important not to complain about the place you're in, but to focus on yourself. Epictetus illustrates this with what we might call "barbecue etiquette" (*Enchiridion,* 1.15):

> Remember that you must behave in life as at a dinner party. Is anything brought around to you? Put out your hand and take your share with moderation. Does it pass by you? Don't stop it. Is it not yet come? Don't stretch your desire towards it, but wait till it reaches you. Do this with regard to children, to a wife, to public posts, to riches, and you will eventually be a worthy partner of the feasts of the gods.

But why bother with the gods' feasts? Why not eat here, today? The choice to eat is within our control, the sausages within our reach (and Epictetus is dead). The important question, then, is: why should we want to discipline ourselves? The answer to this can be found if we imagine ourselves, not at a barbecue, but six feet underground.

What to Do if You Are Buried Alive

Halfway through the movie *Kill Bill II,* the main character is buried alive with a torch inside a coffin. Wonderfully claustrophobic (for those who like that sort of thing) it's also a puzzling scene to run halfway through a film. The main character and the plot seem to hit a dead end. What plausible plot twist could redeem her from this one? A long-lost lover hears her calls and digs her up? She discovers amazing magical powers? She breaks through the coffin with a nail gun hidden in her boot? To advance the plot, it seems, the director is left with little choice but to look very B-grade.

In fact, the director (Quentin Tarantino) inserts the most interesting scene of the whole film. Cutting back ten years, we watch the main character's training in martial arts. On a mountain in China, the beautiful, arrogant American submits to her disciplinarian Yoda Sensei. He sits on her shoulders every day, bashing her with a stick as she breaks her knuckles against wood, punching with only a hand-length between her first and the board. The training takes many years. After this digression back in time, we return to the coffin scene with a new understanding. The main character will be redeemed—by her hard-won martial skills. With the roof of the coffin a hand-length from her nose, she smashes her way through the wood and struggles up through the dirt as it collapses into the coffin. No implausible plot twist required, no magic powers or long-lost lover. Just her willingness, ten years earlier, to submit herself to disciplined training.

We can now define some reasons why we should want to discipline ourselves. Certain sorts of rules—or types of discipline—actually make us more free *over the long run.* If we commit ourselves to training now, over time we'll develop abilities that will give us greater freedom to act. In this case, it means focussing on developing something we can control: our own abilities. The idea goes beyond martial arts. Stoicism's great insight was to apply this mentality to disciplining the emotions. Epictetus wrote: "He who craves or shuns things not under his control can neither be faithful nor free, but must himself be changed and tossed to and fro, and must end by subordinating himself to others."

A Will in Accord with Nature

The single, central, idea of Stoicism is that a good life is one lived "in accordance with nature." In Stoic philosophy, this phrase meant something quite particular, and had nothing to do with living like hippies. (The closest thing to hippies in the Roman Empire were followers of "Epicureanism." This philosophy didn't actually mean "Gorge yourself on food and wine," as we understand it today. In fact, the Epicureans were constantly pointing out that their philosophy was more than just eating, drinking, and ignoring Roman politics. Needless to say, the Romans didn't like it; but Stoicism and Epicureanism were lost to Christianity anyway.)

The Stoics believed that all things in nature are physical and made of fire, turned into different forms by god, the original fire. God is reason, so the world is therefore governed by reason. The human soul comes from that original fire, and thus the soul and human logic are also based in reason. (These are the sorts of conversations the Greeks used to have on verandas.)

This means that, to live in accordance with nature, you need firstly to act in accordance with your own reason. Emotions need to be employed by reason, rather than vice versa. This means training yourself to be in command of your reactions. Emotions (the Greeks called them "passions") are "feelings which happen to you," as opposed to your own chosen actions, which should be rational. Stoics are in control of their emotions. This is the origin of our popular view of Stoicism today: that "Stoic" people are emotionless, tough, and not particularly sympathetic. But this isn't exactly right. The original idea was not that you shouldn't feel anything, but that you shouldn't be psychologically subject to anything. You shouldn't chase after your emotions, or be directed by them; you should act on reason.

When I was young I wondered what the point of *kata* was. It seemed a bit like my sister's horse riding "dressage," when riders would lead horses through some convoluted footwork, to show off, as far as I could tell. No one sat in the grandstands for my *kata*. I tried to explain it to friends who thought it was useless. But *kata* exemplifies the Stoic principle of acting based on controlled reason. *Kata* distil intentioned action to its purest form. Imagine a Stoic philosopher visiting a Karate class (the first proto-Karate classes were a thousand years after the first Stoic classes). He'd understand *kumite*, but what would he make of *kata*? I think he'd see it immediately. A *kata* is a defiant stand against irrational emotion-chasing. It is the highest form of wilfully *chosen* action, a physical logic absorbed by the mind as it is practiced. Epictetus wanted his students to desire the same ideal of clear action, willed by a clear mind.

One technique to practice this was advocated by Zeno of Citium, the founder of Stoicism, who wrote about *apatheia,* or detachment from emotion. The idea was not to ignore emotions, but to notice them, and to moderate them as soon as they start. Unfortunately, we inherit the word "apathy" today. But the detachment from emotion was really meant to be a state of heightened control. Without control, emotions dominate. Cleanthes, Zeno's student, wrote that a man without virtue is "like a dog tied to a cart, and compelled to go wherever it goes." Zeno stressed that emotional control is a discipline to be cultivated. A wise Stoic, instead of being fearful, will be watchful; instead of having desire, will wish; and instead of feeling pleasure, will feel joy. The first, ignoble, feelings arise from lack of emotional discipline; the second, better, feelings result from cultivated emotions. Millennia later, Zeno was echoed by Shotokan Master Gichin Funakoshi, who said that karateka must cultivate the mind and body. As the Stoics knew, this cultivation requires training.

This Stoic worldview fitted together well: the divine fire of reason in god and the universe, and the fire of reason filling human minds. Stoic physics clicked with their idea of logic, which together led to action. Like Karatedo, Stoic philosophy is attractive as a full way of life, a system in which each part is connected to all the other parts. (This attraction may also be the origin of "epistemic vice" in the martial arts: it's good to be Stoic, but the world clearly isn't made of fire.) The corollary of the Stoic's belief in universal reason is that the whole universe is governed by rules. There is no changing these rules. Thus, the second part of "living according to nature" is to accept what nature serves up to you, when it's outside your control. If you're offered steak at the barbecue, don't whinge about the lack of sausages.

Emperor Marcus Aurelius

The Roman Emperor Marcus Aurelius was like President Barack Obama crossed with Master Gichin Funakoshi. He brought together intellect, politics, and practical martial skill. He was known across the Mediterranean as the wise emperor: his life an example of philosophy employed for action. He took the Roman Empire to its peak of power and influence. As a teenager, Aurelius was taught Stoicism, and he followed the teachings throughout his reign. (He wrote that philosophy was his mother, and the government his stepmother: he'd listen politely to one, but really only cared for the other.) Almost two millennia ago, he was thinking about the same idea of "living according to nature" sitting in his tent, on campaign in what is now northern Italy. "Accept the things to which fate binds you, and love the people with whom fate brings you together, but do so with all your heart," he wrote in his diary.

After I took up karate again, I started in a new school at the bottom of the class. Fate had bound me to six-year-olds, who had a higher ranking than me. On one occasion, as we sat on the side watching higher belts perform a *kata*, one of them asked me what belt I was. I was wearing tracksuit pants and T-shirt—my old karategi was now about half my height. I answered "no belt." "What belt do you think you are?" he asked. I thought this was funny and asked him what he thought he was. "I'm white belt," he said, "but I think I'm black belt."

Aurelius would have approved. In his *Meditations* (Kessinger, 2004) he wrote to himself that "you have power over your mind—not outside events. Realize this, and you will find strength." He also wrote that "the secret of all victory lies in the organization of the non-obvious." This is an interesting thought; he was probably referring to the careful organising he was doing with his mind as he wrote notes to himself. Aurelius understood the connection between thought and good action. He thought that nothing should be done rashly, and at random, but "all things according to the most exact and perfect rules of art" (*Meditations*, 4.2).

Aurelius's life tells us something very important: philosophy is not a body of knowledge, but a way of life. Karate, equally, could never be just a body of knowledge: reading about martial arts for years you would never really understand it. For the Stoic, to learn a good way of life was an effort of constant practice and self-reminder. Like muscle movements in Karate, the habits of mind had to become second nature. (Aurelius had a good philosophy for work: "First, begin. To begin is half the work, so half remains. Then, begin this, and you will have almost finished!") The Stoic training was called *askesis*. As well as cultivating emotional control (*apatheia*), the teachers recommended a set of practical exercises to pursue wisdom, courage, moderation, and justice. Writing on anger, Seneca, another Roman Stoic philosopher, wrote:

> Sextius had this habit, that when the day was over and he had retired to his nightly rest, he would put these questions to his soul: "What bad

habit have you cured today? What fault have you resisted? In what respect are you better?" Anger will cease and become more controllable if it finds that it must appear before a judge every day. . . . When the light has been removed from sight, and my wife, long aware of my habit, has become silent, I scan the whole of my day and retrace all my deeds and words. I conceal nothing from myself, I omit nothing. For why should I shrink from any of my mistakes, when I may commune thus with myself?

"See that you never do that again; I will pardon you this time. In that dispute, you spoke too offensively; after this don't have encounters with ignorant people; those who have never learned do not want to learn. You reproved that man more frankly than you ought, and consequently you have not so much mended him as offended him. In the future, consider not only the truth of what you say, but also whether the man to whom you are speaking can endure the truth. A good man accepts reproof gladly; the worse a man is the more bitterly he resents it." (Seneca: Moral and Political Essays, Cambridge University Press, 1995, 3.36.1–4)

Disciplining Love?

As I was finishing an early draft of this chapter, a friend wrote me an email. He liked the idea, but was concerned that love should not be disciplined:

> The feeling of falling in love, by its very nature, is associated with a loss of control. We only fall in love when we do in fact lose ourselves to that emotion and follow it on its path. And this feeling is great—it's actually an example of when most people really enjoy not being free, in the Stoic sense. Discipline love, and you lose a part of the good life.

Other than stopping myself from falling for other people's girlfriends, I think love and discipline aren't total strangers. Some guiding hand must be involved in love because love is an act of communication. It's not enough to just feel the emotion, you need to make it dance with the ebbs and flows of your partner's feelings (like a version of *Kumitachi* sword *kata*). You can't smother your partner—all of the time—and many more subtleties of restraint make love joyful (as opposed to gushing). If not discipline, then this requires gentle control.

Epictetus argued that only a Stoic can really love, because they must distinguish at every stage what is good in a relationship, what is harmful, and what is neither. Stoics can identify *how* to love, not just the fact that they *want* to. In the dojo, good sensei draw on this understanding. My sensei clearly does, particularly when training the young karateka; it seems he holds clearly in his mind what is good about a student, without it interfering with him judging what is bad. He never loses himself to emotion: never irrationally hating bad behaviour, nor heaping on praise.

Karateka do not aim to become robots. The idea is not to drive out emotion with discipline, nor vice versa. The art is in working out the interaction. It is to use your mind to link your emotions with the concerns and imperatives of the world, so you're not just taking a chemical ride on internal hormones. This often means moderating and guiding emotions, but it can also make them deeper, more focused. And in the dojo, much more useful.

An "Act of Will"

We started with the question: What use is discipline outside the dojo? The Stoics answered that a good life is built on self-discipline, and that a lack of discipline doesn't mean freedom, but leads to servitude to damaging emotions. The Stoics would judge people's philosophies by how they behaved; the mark of a Stoic sage was the performance of "acts of will." Wise Stoics know what's best, but they also *do* what's best, with ease. Not only do they recognize that the veranda barbeque is finishing and they should help clean up, but they go to help without forcing themselves. They do it easily; their emotions are light and well-aligned to what they know is good. Their will is virtuous, and their actions follow courageously, confidently, from their will.

Kumite and *kata* both train courageous, confident action. For excellent karateka, right moves flow unconsciously. Training, though, requires conscious acts of will. Paradoxically, in a *kata* there is no allowance made for new movement, but through discipline, karateka learn a skill that is the foundation of true freedom: the ability to act consistently on their will. It's a common idea that having more freedom will lead to a better life. But being free doesn't really guarantee you anything. You need freedom and *ability*—to pursue your goals over weeks, months, and years. This is true freedom: to control the course of your life; not to drift. Karate should remind us that a good life takes a certain type of discipline.

An Enemy Lying in Ambush

Who is the enemy? For Stoics, the enemy was anything that would undermine your internal virtue—those long-practiced habits. By definition then, the enemy could only be internal. This is because it's your choice if you allow external things to cause an internal betrayal of your principles. The same standard applies in Karate. As Funakoshi said: "the ultimate aim of the art of karate lies not in victory or defeat, but in the perfection of the characters of its participants." Karateka do not seek fights. They develop strength by building habits internally, and so the only threat is internal. Sensei Tsutomu Ohshima wrote:

> Each one of us starts Karate with some particular reason: to be a good fighter, to keep in good shape, to protect oneself. I wanted to become very strong myself when I first began. But Karate training soon teaches that real strength is facing oneself strictly, with severe eyes. (*Quotes and Articles, Shotokan Karate Club, University of Washington, Seattle,* website)

My sensei was right, the first step to defeating enemies is discipline. In my teenage years, my enemies were all external. The possibility of embarrassment had to be fought by honing my skills at complicated leg movements. In ancient Athens and Rome, though, teenagers learnt from the Stoics that, in fact, no enemy is external. Epictetus said:

> Philosophy does not promise to secure anything external for man, otherwise it would be admitting something that lies beyond its proper subject-matter. For as the material of the carpenter is wood, and that of statuary bronze, so the subject-matter of the art of living is each person's own life. (*Discourses of Epictetus*, Everyman Paperbacks, 1995, 1.15)

Epictetus says that the Stoic "keeps watch over himself as over an enemy lying in ambush" (*Enchiridion*, 1.48). We are our own enemies—that's the strange conclusion. When we give in to ourselves we become distracted, incoherent. But we shouldn't think of it as an internal war. It's a careful and clear internal tension. The tension of lying in ambush: your mind holding your muscles; your will holding your desires. It's a self-control for something more than its own sake.

As a white belt, trying and failing to hold a *shiko dachi* stance, I had no idea about "veranda philosophy". A free life, for me, continued to mean one without rules. It took a while for me to think about a more satisfying way of growing up. My failure at *shiko dachi* was not just a muscle weakness, but a weakness of will. I'll forgive myself for this one; teenagers are not known for their self-control. But there is a lesson here from a two-thousand-year-old philosophy and a thousand years of martial arts: that when we're called upon to act, it won't just matter how hard we practiced our *kata*, but how many sausages we took at the barbecue.

7

Armbarring the Common Good

SASHA COOPER and TRAVIS TAYLOR

Memories of tussling with a sweaty judoka, struggling to grip, unbalance, and ultimately drive your opponent into the floor: not necessarily the first things we'd recount if some guardian of the afterlife materialised before us.

Faced with such a supernatural arbiter, we might stammer out various justifications for our martial activity. "It brought me glory!" or "I gave my opponent a sense of purpose . . . you know, before I gave him a dislocated shoulder." Our shoelaces might become strangely fascinating.

Assuming the Grim Reaper doesn't turn out to be an ex-samurai (or Don King) we'd need a more sophisticated defense of our bloodlust. Lucky for the judoka, then, that Judo's founder, Jigoro Kano, described ethical development as one of the four main aims of the art, alongside physical and mental improvement, and self-defense.

Kano never claimed to follow a particular school of ethics, preferring his own ideas, which permeate his writings and maxims. But the principles on which he founded them echo an ethical philosophy called utilitarianism, which emerged a generation before Kano was even born.

In 1882, when Kano conceived and developed Judo, Japan was in the throes of an industrial revolution so profound that it transformed the country from a medieval to a modern state within a single generation. As in the Western world, science seemed poised to replace superstition and tradition. The samurai on horseback, with bow and sword, for all their training, would never be a match for revolvers, Gatling guns, and modern artillery.

Jigaro Kano. Image courtesy of The Budokwai, London.

And when I Get Home to You, After the Judo I Do, You Know I Feel Alright

Japanese society was emulating new concepts from the West and discarding customs that had gone unchallenged for hundreds of years—to this day, Japanese schoolboys wear a uniform based on those of nineteenth-century Prussian cadets. Many Japanese knew their country needed to modernize if it was to avoid being exploited or consumed. Some saw anything traditional as anachronistic, to be inevitably replaced by foreign ideas unless it could absorb them on its own terms.

The spirit of the era, throughout the world, was efficiency—eliminating inessential ideas or seeking to unify them by finding an underlying principle. Charles Darwin had just managed to link the entire living population of earth into a single taxonomic tree. Physicists were starting to believe that matter might really be nothing more than vast numbers of identical particles.

Outside the sciences, the ethos was the same—eliminate the unnecessary by using new technologies or proposing new principles. Engineering: an ironclad needed far less construction material to resist cannon fire than a wooden sailing ship. Economics: automation and mechanisation allowed employers to maintain or increase their output while paying far fewer employees. And philosophy: numerous thinkers attempted to remove traditional assumptions from their field—none so unsparingly as the ethicist Jeremy Bentham, an English jurist, born in 1748.

The core of both Kano's and Bentham's philosophies was concise and true to the spirit of efficiency. Bentham saw in England's legal culture a mishmash of archaic ethical principles, many of which contradicted each other. Kano saw in Japan's martial culture an array of techniques and training methods, often taught with a limited understanding of what made them effective. Both men wanted to develop systems that would be more relevant to their modernising societies. To do so they had to define their goal—to understand exactly what their system would achieve if it were followed to the letter. And both men's ultimate goal lay in ethics.

Traditional Jujutsu had a strong moral component in its teaching, but by the Meiji period (1868–1912) it had developed a reputation for being thuggish and unruly—a remnant of pre-modern times unfit for the new age. Kano wanted to eliminate inefficient techniques and find ways to train effectively and safely. But rather than trying to recreate the samurai of old, he sought to create a new breed of martial artist, an ethical champion.

Kano's called the guiding principles of Judo *seiryokuzenyou* and *jitakyouei*. The former is an abbreviation of *seiryoku saizen katsuyo*, which means making the best use of one's personal energy to achieve a goal—more commonly translated as "maximum efficiency." *Jitakyouei* abbreviates *sojo sojou jitakyouei*, which Kano described as meaning that: "The virtues and strengths of one can complement and foster those of another. [This] affords advantages to each of them" (*Mind Over Muscle: Writings from the Founder of Judo*, Kodansha, 2005; p. 71). The usual modern translation is simply "mutual welfare and benefit."

He found that the same principles would serve for both ethical and physical training. *Seiryokuzenyou* is the familiar practice of adapting our technique to the opponent's motion, rather than repeatedly trying a specific throw, while *jitakyouei* is harmony between *tori* (the thrower) and *uke* (the thrown) during *kata*.

Outside the dojo, *jitakyouei* enjoins judoka to put society's welfare above their own, and *seiryokuzenyou* simply encourages efficiency and pragmatism in their efforts to improve that society. Kano's favourite example is a familiar motif (*Mind Over Muscle*, p. 80):

> What is the point of complaining? It is certainly no fun for those who have to listen to the complaints. . . . Rather, all the energy used to complain or grumble should be expended more usefully.

Kano knew that few of us would relish the prospect of training if we were likely to suffer serious injury. But he also realised that *shiai* (competition) against a real opponent would rarely end well if you hadn't practiced your techniques against a partner who was determined to stop you applying them. Kano applied *seiryokuzenyou* to the conflicting demand for safety and effectiveness, and discarded from his syllabus any technique that was too dangerous to practice at full strength.

Strictly speaking, *jitakyouei* and *seiryokuzenyou* aren't separate principles; neither implies anything that could contradict the other. Taken together, the two principles form a compound: each individual in a group should co-operate to maximize its overall benefit in the most efficient way possible.

So Kano's contribution to the history of martial arts (and philosophy) was applying this compound principle to both the ethical and physical realms. But Bentham had laid the groundwork for him by creating, appropriately enough, the most efficient principle that anyone has ever applied to ethics.

Utility Is All You Need

The dominant ethical ideas of the time offered only a series of rules, such as "Don't lie" and "Don't kill." Other approaches offered almost no instruction at all on how you should behave, as long as you had a "virtuous" character.

Bentham thought that a unifying principle was worth any number of rules. He considered daily life, as well as extreme situations: what were people doing that seemed somehow "good" and what made it good? What did saying "thank you" have in common with rescuing children from a burning building—and with not setting fire to orphanages in the first place?

Had he met Kano, Bentham would have analysed Judo slightly differently from its founder. He would have asked *why* it was important to do well in training or competition—it's all very well to give advice that serves equally well to improve your grappling and improve society, but what's the point in doing either?

Utilitarianism is an ultimate answer to these questions—to *all* such questions. Simply put, we should choose any action over the alternatives, when, as Bentham says (in *An Introduction to the Principles of Morals and Legislation*) "the tendency it has to augment the happiness of the community is greater than any it has to diminish it." Rather than happiness, we might say pleasure, positive emotion, "the good," utility (hence "utilitarianism"), or wellbeing, as many who've followed Bentham have done. But to utilitarians, these words are often synonymous. It doesn't matter which you pick.

Bentham wasn't the first person to base ethics on happiness—the Greek philosopher Epicurus had done so over two millennia beforehand—but he was the first to formalize what he called "the principle of utility," the claim that we can judge actions only by the amount of happiness they cause.

Happiness Is a Worn Gi

As for why we should promote happiness rather than, say, virtue, happiness is simply something every one of us values. No one ever complains of being too happy (unless they're worried it won't last). But the value of virtue isn't universal. Just search for the phrase "nice guys finish last" on Google; at the time of writing you get 397,000 hits. Would anyone bemoan "finishing last" if virtue was really its own reward?

Our moral rules, "virtuous" qualities and polite habits usually offer practical ways to increase happiness or prevent suffering—either our own, or more often that of others around us. Bentham gave his advice more poetically to a young girl (*Deontology Together with a Table of the Springs of Action and Article on Utilitarianism*, Oxford University Press, 1983; p. xix):

> Create all the happiness you are able to create; remove all the misery you are able to remove. Every day will allow you, —will invite you to add something to the pleasure of others, —or to diminish something of their pains. And for every grain of enjoyment you sow in the bosom

of another, you shall find a harvest in your own bosom, —while every sorrow which you pluck out from the thoughts and feelings of a fellow creature shall be replaced by beautiful flowers of peace and joy in the sanctuary of your soul.

This might seem optimistic to you twenty-first-century cynics, but it's not so far-fetched. The growing scientific field of happiness studies has revealed various pastimes that make us much better off. Among them are exercise and voluntary work—the epitome of Kano's judo. (You can find more about-happiness studies in Ruut Veenhoven's "Advances in Understanding Happiness", *Revue Québécoise de Psychologie*, 1997.)

And that's the core of utilitarian philosophy, which extends to Judo, Capoeira, Western Boxing, and far beyond, from our daily lives and global politics to our aspirations as both individuals and a species—and still beyond, to any other creature capable of experiencing pleasure or pain. All that matters is the well-being of everyone whose lives we touch, including ourselves.

We practice Judo because it doesn't hurt (much) and we enjoy it. Bentham's principles are visible in Kano's. Taken together, *jitakyouei* and *seiryokuzenyou* seem to dictate a style of martial art that provides the greatest possible benefit from classes; the students try to maximize their learning as efficiently and safely as possible. It might seem prone to causing the occasional injury, but Kano thought safety at least as important as skill.

So Kano maximized the happiness judoka gain from pulling off a perfect technique against a resisting opponent by removing any technique that couldn't be practiced safely in full-resistance *randori*. Kano mightn't have been thinking in purely utilitarian terms when he created Judo, but he accepted the comparison. In an article he wrote in 1925, discussing Bentham and his students, Kano said "If people think their ideas are close to mine, let it be so. I don't mind." ("On Various Questions about Jita-Kyoei," *Sakko*, May 1925.)

We might also practice Judo for self-defense, but to a utilitarian this comes to the same thing as utility. In learning to avoid being mugged, we prevent ourselves from experiencing negative happiness, more commonly called suffering. Probability matters rather than certainty. Statisticians would say we increase our *expected* happiness by suffering a little more from training harder now in return for increasing our chances in a real fight that we might never experience. Of course, judoka might say harder training is more fun anyway.

Bentham's Lonely Hearts Club Band

But can we simply add up or subtract different kinds of pleasure or pain? This idea has certainly caused controversy. Bentham believed that all conscious states were ultimately positive or negative contributions to a single sum. A dislocated shoulder, physical exhaustion, or fear of death—all that matters about these experiences is how much they subtract from the sum of happiness. Similarly, elation at winning a competition and relaxing with an ice-cream after intense training just make us happier by different amounts.

Bentham went so far as to propose a calculus for happiness. This is a way to compare factors like the duration, purity, extent,

Jeremy Bentham. Image courtesy of the Bentham Project, University College London.

intensity, and probability of pleasures, to decide which to pursue. In practice we can never calculate the exact difference between two examples of happiness, any more than we can calculate the exact probability of a particular throw working in competition; however, just as we can still believe that one throw will be more likely to work than another, we can also expect something to do more harm than good, or vice versa. For example we probably expect that the pleasure we find in practicing martial arts outweighs the harm from bruises we'll also gain along the way. If we didn't think so, why would we train?

To some people, such a simple approach is self-evidently wrong; the pain of a training injury is fundamentally different from the joy of success – after all, you can experience both at the same time without them cancelling each other out. But Bentham never believed that such things *felt* similar, he simply believed that they were quantifiable by the amount we like or loathe them.

Nothing You Can Say but You Can Learn How to Play the Game. It's Easy

Many people disliked utilitarianism's potential to justify horrific acts if they make enough people happy. (An opportunistic Roman might have tried to justify feeding Christians to the lions on such grounds.) In reply, Bentham's protégé John Stuart Mill emphasized that we could follow secondary principles, rules of thumb, which we can choose by imagining how much happiness the rule itself will provide.

For example, when martial artists step on the mat, we usually obey the rules of our style, no matter how much we want to win. These rules might mean we don't beat up white belts even "for their own good." They also allow us to react faster. When someone taps to an arm-bar we release the pressure immediately, rather than trying to calculate whether the happiness we might gain from ensuring it's on will outweigh their potential suffering.

But these rules aren't divine—they come directly from our aim of increasing happiness. Occasionally, following them will obviously do more harm than good . . . in which case we won't. But they're useful guidelines for our behavior. "To inform a traveller respecting the place of his ultimate destination," Mill observed, "is not to forbid the use of landmarks and direction-posts on the way" ("Utilitarianism," in *John Stuart Mill and Jeremy Bentham: Utilitarianism and Other Essays*, Penguin, 1987; p. 296).

Subsequent philosophers would call this kind of view *rule utilitarianism* and Bentham's version *act utilitarianism*. The debate over the two views continues to this day.

Don't Carry the World upon Your Shoulders. Only Your Opponent

Seeking the best for society turns out to be a daunting task. For us to really maximize happiness, we'd have to work all day for as much money as possible, and donate everything we didn't need for survival to the most efficient humanitarian charity we could find. Why should we follow an ethical system that demands the impossible of us?

In the vision Kano had for martial arts, we can find a realistic solution to utilitarianism's demands. He never demanded that his students become physical champions. *Jitakyouei* was more important to him than any individual's success in *shiai*. Following Kano's teachings wholeheartedly won't make a student invincible, it would only improve them—but in every sense. Kano's philosophy isn't necessarily all-or-nothing, and neither is utilitarianism. Judo and utilitarianism aren't about success or failure, they're about continual improvement.

All judoka know the pain of *randori* against a far superior opponent. We mess up, and then we try to improve. Maybe we do it for self-defense, exercise, or because we love a challenge. We enjoy the sense of improvement, and of effort well spent, so we put in as much time and effort as we can. We might still seek to train harder and longer, but ultimately we feel good about what we have done, not guilty about what we haven't. It would be a dull sport if we could perfect it in a day. Similarly, if maximizing happiness seems like a daunting task, it's only because the alternatives are so easy.

On the other hand, if all sensei demanded that we dominate the mat every time we stepped onto it lest they expel us from their *dojo*, we would never improve our Judo. We'd quit on the first day. No-one would follow any philosophy that demanded impossible dedication. So instead, we do the exercise we can, and put in the time or the money we can to important causes. Neither needs to be a sacrifice. Indeed both can be deeply satisfying.

And in the end, if these philosophies give us more to worry about than others, it's only because they also give us more to feel happy about.

8
Sparring with Emptiness

KEVIN KREIN

When you look long into an abyss, the abyss also looks into you.

—FRIEDRICH NIETZSCHE, *Beyond Good and Evil*

When the clouds of bewilderment clear away, there is the true void.

—MIYAMOTO MUSASHI, *The Book of Five Rings*

I've studied Karate for just over fifteen years. This isn't very long by some standards, but my martial-arts training has played a key role in my conception of who I am, what my goals are, and what I expect to accomplish. This is also true for many of those I train with. My question in this chapter is why people like us find the study of martial arts so rewarding, and meaningful.

Developing martial skills does not, on its own, provide a satisfactory answer to this question. There are certainly people who study martial arts because they have to fight. Some may work in ice factories fronting for drug smuggling operations run by Big Bosses; or may even be invited, from time-to-time, to remote islands on which secret tournaments are held by shady millionaires up to no good; and some, of course, may feel the need to develop fighting and self-defense skills because they fantasize about finding themselves in such situations.

But I teach philosophy at a small university in a relatively crime-free area. My world is pretty peaceful and, if I am honest, defending myself from a physical attack is not much of a concern. And I've never been invited to a secret no-holds-barred kumite at a super-villain's island headquarters.

Even if I did need to fight, Karate seems a poor investment of my time and energy. Sure, I learn some combat skills. But spending decades refining techniques makes little sense, next to other self-defense options. For pure self-defense, a short course combined with carrying a practical self-defense weapon, such as mace, would be a much better use of my time. In fact, just staying away from crime or danger would be the best solution—spending years learning kata and developing precise techniques seems wasteful and clumsy from the standpoint of efficiency.

Another way that people attempt to explain their devotion to martial arts is to appeal to the connection between martial arts and Buddhism, particularly Zen. Practicing martial arts requires full attention and trains you to maintain a certain relaxed, though focussed, state of mind. Thus, it's rightfully described as a type of do-zen or moving meditation. There are serious martial artists who are Buddhists and I do not want to criticize their conception of Buddhism or the martial arts.

But many practitioners who study martial arts seriously, including some philosophers, find Buddhism a bit cumbersome. Notions such as rebirth and karma, which are central to Buddhist teaching, may not appeal to martial artists who are not religiously inclined.

I take a different view of why the study of the martial arts can play a significant role in practitioners' lives, a view which depends on neither religion nor self-defense. Traditional martial arts, such as Karate, provide a framework for living a meaningful life in a world that lacks objective meaning. In other words, martial arts fit particularly well with the existentialist understanding of the human condition. The study of a martial art can be a very valuable addition to the lives of people who are concerned about living a meaningful life.

The Existentialist Starting Point

The existentialist worldview is the result, in part, of the success and development of science and technology. As we gained knowledge of the size and scope of the universe, it became increasingly clear that we were not the center of it.

Nineteenth-century existentialist philosopher Friedrich Nietzsche describes human existence as it appears from a big-picture perspective:

In some remote corner of the universe, poured out and glittering in innumerable solar systems, there was once a star on which clever animals invented knowledge. That was the highest and most mendacious minute of "world history"—yet only a minute. After nature had drawn a few breaths the star grew cold, and the clever animals had to die.

One might invent such a fable and still not have illustrated sufficiently how wretched, how shadowy and flighty, how aimless and arbitrary, the human intellect appears in nature. There have been eternities when it did not exist; and when it is done for again, nothing will have happened. (*The Portable Nietzsche*, Penguin, 1976, p. 42)

We may view our intellectual capacities, or the power and grace of our spinning back kicks, as very special. But from the perspective Nietzsche presents, human action is meaningless—just a tiny, powerless, transient part of a big, indifferent cosmos.

God isn't watching, in other words—in fact, he's nowhere to be seen.

From the seventeenth century onward, modern science explained more and more aspects of our world. In addition to developing more complex and useful machines, science provided explanations of the motion of the earth and planets, of health and disease, and of human behavior. Writing of what he calls the death of God, Nietzsche claims that the implications of the loss of the conception of God as an active participant in the universe have not yet been generally understood:

The event itself is far too great, too distant, too remote from the multitude's capacity for comprehension even for the tidings of it to be thought of as having *arrived* as yet. Much less may one suppose that many people know as yet *what* this event really means—and how much must collapse now that this faith has been undermined because it was built upon this faith, propped up by it, grown into it; for example, the whole of our European morality. (*The Gay Science*, Vintage, 1974, p. 279)

Part of being an effective martial artist is perceiving the nature of an opponent's movements early on. In the same way, part of being a great philosopher lies in seeing implications of intellectual positions early on. One of Nietzsche's most insightful contributions to the history of philosophy was to see, early on, the implications of a scientific worldview. By the late nineteenth century, there was already little room for God in our life—as a result, his influence waned. Nietzsche's claim was not just that God is dead, but also that the true implications of that death had not yet been recognized but are deeply upsetting. And these conditions are those that gave birth to existentialism: a cosmos where God was dead, or KO'd.

Through the twentieth century, Jean-Paul Sartre came to be recognized as the most prominent existentialist philosopher. In *Existentialism and Human Emotion* (Citadel, 1985), Sartre claims that, "Existentialism is nothing else than an attempt to draw all the consequences of a coherent atheistic position" (p. 51). Both Sartre and Nietzsche agree that without God there can be no moral system that exists independently of human creation. And thus, we have nothing to appeal to if we wish to condemn or justify human actions.

But perhaps the most significant consequence of the absence of God, according to Sartre, is that human beings have no essential nature. If there is no God, what we are supposed to *be* is not determined. As conscious beings, humans determine what they are, and what it is to be a human, through choices and actions. In Sartrean terms, as human beings, our existence precedes our essence— humans come into existence, and then determine what their essence is. This is the existentialist starting point then: as fully conscious human beings, we are alone. Human existence is meaningless, there are no values to appeal to in determining our actions, and we have no essential nature beyond what we create. Like soldiers who are abandoned with no hope of victory, we can continue to fight, but our action will not affect any final outcome.

Freedom, Transcendence, and Responsibility

Is it possible, once we have accepted these stark truths, to live a life that is fulfilling? One point to notice is that if our existence precedes our essence, as Sartre claims, we freely create ourselves through our choices and actions. We are only fully human then, when we are exercising our ability to define and redefine ourselves. Human consciousness, Sartre argues, is constantly striving to transcend itself—that is, to overcome itself. We choose our own projects and goals and, through our attempts to achieve them, we transcend who we are and redefine ourselves.

Here, we return to the martial arts. Martial arts provide a lifetime of opportunities for self-improvement. The study of a traditional martial art provides a framework in which to situate one's continual development as a human being. The emphasis on striving for perfection of both mind and body make the dojo an ideal place to continue to recreate ourselves by going beyond our current understanding and abilities.

There is no God, and ultimately no meaning to human existence, according to the existentialist understanding of the world. So, there is no independent universal standard against which one can measure oneself. But one of the beauties of martial arts traditions is that they do not need to appeal to such standards. When a student performs a kata, the grace and power of the movements are apparent and contained within the kata itself. Balance, control, form, and power are directly evident and one need not go beyond the system itself to identify the quality of performance.

But isn't this stifling or inflexible? Indeed, one possible criticism of this approach is that it does not afford opportunities for students to develop their *own* versions of themselves they're filling molds, rather than crafting their own.

While this objection seems compelling, it ignores the importance of individual experience. While students *are* given rigid instructions early in their training, they must eventually adapt their techniques to their own body, mindset and circumstances. It is not only *possible* to transcend oneself while training in the martial arts, it is required.

Accepting that we create ourselves through our choices and actions can be daunting, Sartre argues that the image we create "is valid for everybody and for our whole age" (p. 17). We define, not only who we are as individuals, but what it is to be human. In our choices and actions, we are responsible to all of mankind.

This sounds a little abstract, but it's a perfectly everyday phenomenon. We feel this burden, in a practical sense, as members of any group. As a group member, an individual's actions help to define the character of the group. For example, if I am the member of a dojo and bribe judges in order to win tournaments, then, in a very straightforward way, my dojo is a dojo that includes cheaters. The dojo is no longer an honest dojo. In the same way, if a human being becomes, for example, a serial killer, then what it is to be a human is to be the kind of being that sometimes kills several other people. When I act, I act *as* a human being. Thus, what I do is what human beings do—or, at least, what they *can* do. When we choose, we choose *what it is to be human*. This is a serious burden and responsibility.

We may also feel this weight in a more ideal sense. Sartre argues that "there is not a single one of our acts which does not at the same time create an image of man as we think he ought to be" (p. 17). When I act on the basis of my conscious choices, I act as I think that I should, given my situation. At the same time, I am a human being and see myself as such. In this way, we are all moral standards; we are all quietly saying: *I* am what it is to be a human being, and *all* should do as I do.

We cannot escape our freedom or responsibility. And we have nothing to fall back on, in our choices. When difficult moral choices arise, we *must* act, and acting defines who we are, but we cannot wait for God, or the universe, to offer solutions. There are no objective moral standards to justify our lives. In Sartre's terms, we cannot pass beyond our own subjectivity; beyond the small, situated perspectives we have.

Bad Faith and Authenticity

As Sartre puts it, "man is condemned to be free" (p. 23). We are thrust into existence, and whatever we do determines who and what we are. In addition to freedom humans may not want, humans also have responsibility that cannot be escaped. Sartre claims that those who are not honest with themselves are in "bad faith" (*mauvaise foi*). Because, on his view, there are no universal moral standards, Sartre cannot point to an objective reason why one should be honest with oneself. But he can and does point to the dangers of bad faith, the most serious of which is the failure to live authentically. The opposite of bad faith is authenticity, living in full awareness and acceptance of one's freedom. For Sartre, at least, human life is only truly fulfilling when authentic transcendence is achieved—by this, he means a life of conscious, deliberate, honest striving, rather than blame, cowardice and willing ignorance.

Here martial arts can play a significant role. For those who are already inclined to accept the existentialist position, the study of martial arts helps characterize and accept an unclouded view of the human condition. According to both Nietzsche and Sartre, it takes an enormous amount of courage to act in the face of such philosophical realizations. Martial-arts training is designed to help students develop the ability to courageously act as individuals. It should also help them to face situations with clarity, even when stress and distractions are present.

While sparring in the martial arts, we are confronted with other humans who approach and attack, and are expected, in addition to defending ourselves, to attack our opponents. The resulting physical interaction can be very stressful. At the same time, we are expected to remain calm and in control of ourselves. The idea of remaining calm in such situations is not new. In *The Book of Five Rings* (Overlook Press, 1974), Musashi writes of facing opponents: "Both in fighting and in everyday life you should be determined though calm. Meet the situation without tenseness yet not recklessly, your spirit settled yet unbiased" (p. 53). This is not easy to accomplish. But one could expect that a person of this character would be more able to accept difficult truths about themselves, and their situation.

That's not to say that all people who are good at fighting have a clear understanding of themselves and the world, or are in a position to achieve Sartre's authentic transcendence. It's obvious that this is not the case. And studying a martial art is clearly not the only path to authenticity. My point is that studying a martial art provides a very good opportunity to develop the kinds of skills required for authentic transcendence.

For example, when things work right in the dojo, students acquire the ability to focus on situations rather than their anxieties, desires, or anger. Often, the intricacy of the techniques blocks out anything but the kata they are performing, or the opponent they're facing. The more you become accustomed to this state of mind, the easier it is to focus in this way. One of the significant practical benefits of martial arts study is having the ability to be aware of situations and what they require without self-conscious interference or distortion.

This can translate into a certain type of philosophical honesty as well. Sartre maintains that accepting one's freedom and responsibility requires courage. Those who are accustomed to making assessments with focused attention have tools that can help them, when they are applied correctly, to attend to, assess, and accept, philosophical positions, even if those positions are uncomfortable and threatening. Fighters make better philosophers.

It may only be "philosophical'" martial artists who ask questions about the nature and meaning of their existence. Those who do, however, will have tools they can implement to help them honestly and sincerely confront their lives.

Owning Our Actions

So, martial arts can lead to courage and clarity. But they can also enhance our sense of responsibility. If our essence depends on our choices and actions, we can't defer to some underlying human nature. And we can't refer to anything other than our choices, decisions, achievements. It would not make sense, then, for me to explain away a cowardly choice or immoral action by referring to my innate cowardice, or the sin I inherited from Adam. And I cannot say: "I could've been a great fighter, but I was never invited to the secret death match on the island." I am what I am, and any hidden, undeveloped talents are non-existent. I have to freely, boldly, and with clear eyes, claim responsibility for what I've done, and who I am.

Martial arts can help with this. In a martial art such as Karate, our actions stand on their own. In sparring, for instance, we either score points or do not. In general, except for the purposes of improvement, excuses are neither asked for nor accepted. Students either perform well or they do not. It would make little sense for a martial artist to claim that he or she knows a particular kata, but has never had ample time to practice, so cannot actually perform it. The Sartrean martial artist claims that knowledge of a technique is nothing other than the ability to demonstrate it. Until the student performs well, it does not makes sense to refer to his or her abilities. And this goes for most martial arts: the existentialist position is actually garden variety knowledge for most practitioners.

Acting Without Hope

As well as taking full responsibility for our actions, we must be honest about our power: we can only see, do, and know so much. We're free, but within limits. I can, to some degree, estimate the immediate effects of my own actions. In the case of those people I know, I can also guess what to expect from them. But, beyond what my experience can tell me, it's impossible to predict the behavior of humans in general. Sartre fought in the French resistance, spent time as a prisoner in a Nazi camp, was strongly opposed to fascism, and actively supported Communism for most of his life. Considering his own case, he claimed that no matter what causes we choose to support, we cannot be sure that others will continue our work or destroy it:

> Given that men are free and that tomorrow they will freely decide what man will be, I can not be sure that after my death, fellow-fighters will carry on my work to bring it to its maximum perfection. Tomorrow, after my death, some men may decide to set up Fascism, and others may be cowardly and muddled enough to let them do so. If so, Fascism will then be the human reality, so much the worse for us. (p. 31)

We cannot see the ultimate meaning or worth of our actions. Sartre claims that this is the meaning of the existentialist claim that we should act without hope. It is not that we don't expect that things might go the way we wish, but that we accepts that we *cannot know this.*

Martial artists, however, *know* that their actions might be futile and often accept this fact of life. Because doing well in a martial art requires full concentration on your current action, when you've decided to act, the focus must be on the action, not the long-term effects of it. And when you enter a combat situation, you must also recognize the possibility of injury or death. A tentative, cautious attitude can be a dangerous way to fight. When you're sparring in Karate, attacking often means closing a gap and putting yourself in a place that's vulnerable to attack as well. Acting without hope is as much a part of the martial arts as it is of existentialism.

Living the Absurd Life

If Sartre and Nietzsche are right, there is no objective set of values against which we may measure ourselves. We may adopt ideals, but if we are consistent we must admit that they are of our own creation. At the same time, we're responsible for our choices and actions, and there are no excuses for what we choose to do. Thus, existentialists generally hold that human existence is absurd. We find ourselves living, interacting, and believing, for no justifiable reason. We think of ourselves and our actions as being very important, but ultimately, our actions have no meaning in any frameworks other than those we create and adopt.

Perhaps the greatest value of the martial arts is that they provide a response to the absurdity of human existence. If I and other students of the martial arts did live in violent environments in which we could expect to be attacked by, or have to attack, other human beings, then the use of tasers, pepper spray, and handguns might be more a part of our training. Instead, in the dojo in which I train, the focus is on traditional empty hand skills. We follow a traditional hierarchy and wear traditional uniforms. Much of what we do is not obviously connected to contemporary life and culture. The fact that we spend years trying to improve and perfect a particular series of movements in a kata really is difficult to explain. But, it is in its disconnectedness to anything but self-development that we find the true value of the study of martial arts.

While I'm not overly concerned about being attacked, I am concerned about living a fulfilling life.

I appreciate knowing that if I am in a self-defense situation, need to guard a nightclub door, or find myself at a brutal island tournament, I have the requisite skills. But this is not why I have spent years studying Karate. In the face of a world without meaning, I want to consciously and authentically make choices that cultivate, develop and refine my existence. I study Karate because it provides a structure for this, and offers skills to aid this pursuit.

Martial arts in their highest form are concerned with self-development for its own sake. Anyone who sees the human condition from an existentialist perspective, and commits himself or herself to pursuing perfection through the martial arts, does so in heroic defiance of the absurdity of life.

9

Grrrl in a Gi

PATRICIA PETERSEN

> To become a feminist is to develop a radically altered consciousness of oneself.
>
> —SANDRA BARTKY, *Femininity and Domination*

When I was a teenager, a jealous male acquaintance told me he intended to rape and kill me. "*Not* shaping up to be one of my better days," I thought. Fourteen hours of fighting later, a middle finger bitten off (his), he also had multiple facial cuts and black eyes. He had not succeeded.

Around the same time, I became aware of feminist concerns, such as voting rights, women's right to bodily integrity and autonomy, abortion and reproductive rights, protection from domestic violence, sexual harassment and rape, workplace rights, including maternity leave and equal pay.

In my mid-twenties, I went off to university and studied feminism. I learnt that the first wave of feminism, mainly concerned with voting rights, was in the nineteenth and early twentieth centuries; that the second, which focused on legal and social equality, was in the 1960s and 1970s; and that the third, a reaction to the perceived failures of second-wave feminism, began in the 1990s. I discovered that feminist theory emerged from these feminist movements and that power was central to it.

I identified myself as a feminist. I announced to others that I was a feminist. But I wasn't one. Not really. I was dependent on man, and had an ironic willingness to tolerate violence in romantic relationships.

In some important respects, I was a doormat, and, as a result, suffered terribly from depression. What caused this vulnerability? Who knows? At the end of the day, it seemed much more important to deal with it than understand what had led to it.

The Black Belt

I did address it, and, in so doing, became a feminist. When? Not on any particular day, certainly not overnight, but gradually over many years. How? Undergoing therapy? Reading about and being exposed to feminist doctrines? Raising awareness of violence towards women? Joining feminist groups?

No. I'd tried these and, although they were helpful, none of them was a cure; none of them markedly changed my underlying predispositions to behave or my personality.

What was successful was learning the art of Karatedo. Developing Karate skills, the emphasis of which was on respect—for self and others—magically sharpened and altered the perception I had of myself, and the world in which I lived.

By the time I was presented with a black belt, I felt like a feminist and acted like one. I'd learnt that Karate and feminism belong together; that Karate, with its mysterious and at times subtle teachings, had driven me to become a feminist—a real one.

Hold on! Before you mentally replay scenes from *Lara Croft: Tomb Raider, Charlie's Angels: Full Throttle*, or *Crouching Tiger, Hidden Dragon*, let's get clear about how I changed. I never—unfortunately—developed the camera-enhanced on-screen fighting skills of Ange and Cam, and if I attempted a double summersault with side-kick, I'd end up in a spinal ward. But what I *do* know is how to reduce the risk of violence; I am repelled by abusive relationships; I am no longer relationship-dependent; and when regularly training, don't experience any mental "downs."

And were Mr Fingerless to show up one day, and insist on another round, it wouldn't take anything like fourteen hours to remove his most prized digit.

To be a feminist, one has to become one. Being a feminist goes beyond the "political"; it cuts across the ideological divisions within the women's movement. It involves feminist changes in behaviour. A woman who becomes a feminist will behave like one.

The author, ready for another round

Two-Year-Old versus Patriarchy

Imagine a world in which all women and girls were karataka—a planet composed of females who started Karate training at the age of two, and who continued training diligently and conscientiously until old-age. (I've taught karate to a two-year-old; I know that it's possible for very young females to train.) What would such a world be like?

Would women be safe from domestic violence? Sexual assault? Would young girls be protected from abduction? Would women be more vocal in the workplace and demand better working conditions? Push for promotion? Would they more often tell men to do their own washing, clean the loo, and darn their own socks? Would they need to tell them?

Well, let's first explore what life for women is currently and really like. In Australia, where conditions for women are significantly better than in developing and newly industrializing countries:

- **1 in 4 women is exposed to domestic violence**

- **200 women are sexually assaulted every day**

- **women's total average earnings are 66 per cent of men's**

- **women are mainly in part-time work due to family responsibilities**

- **only 38 per cent of women are covered by paid maternity leave**

- **tax benefits favour stay-at-home mothers but provide no assistance for those who wish to work**

- **women do at least 65 per cent of unpaid household labor and around 75 per cent of childcare.** (*Violence Against Women in Australia*: <www.aic.gpv.au/publications/rpp/06/RPP06.pdf>. *Statistical Information: Australian Centre for the Study of Sexual Assault*: <www.aifs.gov.au/acssa/statistics.html>)

Laws mandating the reporting of domestic violence are now in place in all states of the US. Statistics reveal that women experience significantly more partner violence than men:

- **25 percent of surveyed women, compared with 8 percent of surveyed men, said they were raped or physically assaulted by a current or former spouse, cohabiting partner, or date in their lifetime**

- **1.5 percent of surveyed women and 0.9 percent of surveyed men said they were raped and/or physically assaulted by such a perpetrator in the previous 12 months**

- **approximately 1.5 million women and 834,700 men are raped and/or physically assaulted by an intimate partner annually in the United States.** (*Facts about Violence*: <*www.feminist.com/antiviolence/facts.html*>. *Bureau of*

Justice, Crime, and Victim Statistics: <*www.ojp.usdoj .gov/bjs/cvict.html*>. *Department of Justice's Office on Violence Against Women:* <*www.ovw.usdoj .gov*>. *Rape, Abuse, and Incest National Network:* <*www.rainn.org/ statistics*>.)

At the UN's Pan Pacific Southeast Asia Women's Association Twenty-First International Conference in 2001, it was pointed out that in the world as a whole:

- **women comprise 51% of the population, but do 66% of the work**

- **receive 10% of the income**

- **and own less than 1% of the property.** (*Pan Pacific Southeast Asia Women's Association:* <www.ppseawa.org>)

Not the post-feminist utopia of the sort that's being widely proclaimed in popular women's magazines and newspapers!

So we've now had several waves of feminism (including the fourth wave that some feminists suggest we entered about 2000), widespread public acknowledgement of women's rights, tales from the celebrity woman "having-it-all" (and making superwoman look like an underachiever) where nothing is impossible and nothing is closed to her. All these trends, educational opportunities, expectations and supports, and we still have these statistics, even for "first world" countries like Australia and the US.

Given how difficult it apparently is for women to make structural changes which will benefit themselves, and the resilience individual women seem to demonstrate in respect of not making choices which will benefit them, what can Karate do for women, for feminism? And is learning Karate compatible with feminism? With all forms of it?

Yes. Every feminist, regardless of when they were born, or what doctrine of feminist thought they subscribe to, considers it desirable that women are empowered, are provided with skills and support, in order to successfully deal with patriarchal abuse, be that physical or psychological. Karate, when learned in a good dojo, can crystallize awareness of male forms of abuse and impart the tools necessary to ward off unwanted contact with and attention from men.

Self-Defense

But how does it work? Well, most obviously, it teaches you to defend yourself if ever necessary. You are not going to learn to do this by just hearing about it, but here are a few tips anyway.

- **The best way of warding off harm is to avoid it in the first place. (If your Karate school doesn't stress this, get out of there!)**

- **Never underestimate your attacker. Always assume he's dangerous.**

- **Seek to deliver your striking actions to the attacker's anatomical weak points (eyes, nose, groin, knees) rather than hard, resistant areas (upper arms, thighs).**

- **After delivering the striking action to your attacker's target area, don't lose sight of him. Be constantly aware of the possibility of continuation of attack.**

- **Get away from your attacker as soon as possible.**

"Hold on a minute,"—you may be thinking—"I'm not that pretty, sexy, or young. I don't need martial arts, all that training. No one is going to attack me." Don't be fooled. Whether you are beautiful, plain, young or old, as a woman you are not immune from attacks. There's no guarantee that your name won't join tomorrow's multitude of crime statistics recorded in daily papers.

"Okay,"—you think, "I'll go off and learn martial arts for a couple of weeks. There are some very short courses in self-defense mastery that promise complete safety under any and all circumstances. I'll enrol in one of these." Warning. Develop a false sense of confidence as a result of these teachings and you could end up in hospital, or worse, the mortuary.

However, being exposed to Karate techniques and teachings at a reputable dojo and gaining your black belt, over a long period of time, can teach you self-defense for the rest of your life.

"But surely,"—you may be thinking, "no amount of forward planning can prepare a woman ahead of a rape attack. Fear will determine how a woman will react. Fear kicks in, and what happens from there is just response. Fear will cause some women to run, some will fight and some will freeze."

No. Karate not only toughens you up physically, it strengthens you mentally. It teaches you that you need not be paralyzed by fear if confronted by an attacker. Black belt women have spent hours, weeks, years, training, learning not to experience fear when faced with danger.

The author, facing danger with a haughtily raised eyebrow

You and Your Mind

Fine. But how does learning to kick, punch, and block transform you into a feminist? How does it nurture your sense of feminist justice? Aid self-development? Allow you to be relationship-independent? Deal with sexual harassment? Surely it merely teaches you to fight, right? Wrong! The answer, again, is your mind.

Karate is a martial art developed by people who were prohibited the use of weapons, making it a defensive art. When you're attacked, empty hands (which the word *karate* implies) are sufficient to defend oneself if you are accomplished in the art. However, to become highly skilled takes discipline, both physical and mental.

Because of the mental emphasis required in Karate training, your mind becomes sharp and strong; you become mentally solid and hard, not just when doing Karate, and not merely when you perhaps need to respond to an assailant, but in your everyday dealings with others, your relationships with others. Karate is a way of life.

A good black belt female is mentally tough. No sexual harassment. No put-downs. No bad relationships. No crap.

Research involving participant-observation and thirty in-depth interviews with women who practice Seido karate at Thousand Waves, a feminist martial arts dojo in Chicago, showed that a woman's self concept is profoundly altered when a physically empowering activity such as Karate is practiced (Sharon Guthrie, "Liberating the Amazon: Feminism and the Martial Arts," *Women and Therapy* 16, pp. 107–119.) It also indicated that healing from incest, rape, and other forms of violence, is facilitated by martial arts or self-defense training in ways that are qualitatively different from psychological therapy. This suggests that approaches that empower women physically, as well as mentally and spiritually, are more effective in producing personal and social change than cognitive strategies alone.

Having a black belt isn't something that you put on and take off—it's with you at every event; it's on you in every situation. As a female black belt, aware of your feminist rights, you take your black belt with you, to every encounter with every man in every context. In fact, it becomes so integral to who you are, the consciousness you have of yourself, that it's virtually impossible to take it off.

The Other Side

So far so good. But if we left things there, you would have a very one-sided picture of things. We've had the yang. Now let's have the yin. Paradoxically, Karate does not teach you to be violent. For a start, as far as self-defense goes, the most important lesson is: don't be there. If you sense any danger, get away from it. Good Karate training teaches you to use violence only when no other choice. Only when it is impossible to get away from an attacker, should you stay and fight.

There are of course Karate teachers (*sensei*) and dojos which don't emphasize defensive tactics and skills. They may also expose women to patronizing, sexist, language and behaviors, which don't focus on making girls and women physically and mentally strong.

Female students of these teachers and dojos might own a black pieces of cloth that they tie around themselves during training, but they don't look, act, or speak like black belts. Only if something looks like a duck, waddles like a duck, quacks like a duck, is it a duck. They aren't really black belts if they aren't independent, self-possessed, and can demonstrate that they have "guts."

Ethics and Respect

But there's a lot more to it than that. Suppose that you do have to defend yourself physically. Do you inflict maximal damage? Certainly not. There is a myriad of ethical rules surrounding the practice of Karate. Karate teaches you that respect is just as important as courage.

A fellow sits next to you on the bus. There's no one other than you and the guy on the bus, and you feel uncomfortable. You move to another seat. He follows you and sits next to you again and attempts to talk to you. You feel more uncomfortable. As a black belt, how do you deal with this situation?

You are aware of your right to sit on your own if you choose to do so, and that there is a need to say or do something. After all, he is in your space and you don't want him there. As a black belt, you aren't going to allow him to sit close to you at your own expense. So how do you respond?

Punch his head, break his nose, and then when he's writhing in pain spit at him that he's a "loser" and that he "needs to get a life"? No! The guy is a pain in the butt; he's not Ted Bundy! You have respect, respect for self, respect for others. Avoid violence, and never use more physical force than is absolutely necessary. Karate also teaches you that there's a difference between being assertive and aggressive. Making sarcastic comments and put-downs in this context won't leave your self-respect intact. However, being assertive ensures that you demonstrate respect for yourself and the person to whom you are speaking. Being verbally aggressive is indicative of loss of control and weakness; being verbally assertive demonstrates control and strength.

"I'm feeling uncomfortable with you sitting next to me. I'd like to sit on my own," is probably all this is required for the guy to move. If he doesn't change seats, you can move again and say firmly: "As I said, I'd like to sit on my own." Your sense of self-confidence, your tone of voice, the fact that you're in control, means that the guy will probably leave you alone. Unless he attempts to touch you, there is no need to use physical force at all.

Not everything is solved with a kick to the head—but it's good to keep practicing

Care of the Self

Some women might tolerate feeling uncomfortable and begrudgingly choose to spend what could have been a pleasant bus trip being forced to chat, despite understanding feminist doctrines and theories. Why? Because society has taught them from a young age that men's needs, desires, wants, should eclipse their own. Even though they believe in feminism, they haven't nurtured or attended to what the French philosopher, Michel Foucault, refers to as the "care of the self" (*Care of the Self*, Vintage Books, 1990).

They haven't engaged in activities, methods and techniques ("tools"), or what Foucault also calls "practices of the self," that develop ethical self-understanding and discovery that allow for feminist notions to be put into practice, to lead to feminist action. Of course, for Foucault, as subjects in the world, going about our business, engaging in activities, we are constantly defining who we are, our psychological maps and dispositions to behave. The black belt female refuses to buy into what should be considered outdated and inappropriate societal expectations of women. Why should she put up with anyone invading her space? Whey should she privilege his feelings over her own? So what if he feels rejected? Embarrassed? That's his problem. Provided she's respectful, assertive and not aggressive, why shouldn't she feel comfortable? Why shouldn't she enjoy her bus trip?

For Foucault, "practices of the self" or forms of knowledge and strategies, allow individuals to transform themselves in order to achieve a certain state of happiness, wisdom, strength, and self-respect. This understanding of how the self is susceptible to change helps us understand how women who learn Karate increasingly gain power through knowledge—they come to understand their strengths and weaknesses, embrace weaknesses in order to over-come them, develop, with the help of their teachers, their physical and mental strength and stamina. By the time they are black belts, they have been exposed to "tools" which have taught them to value and respect themselves—they have learnt how to ensure that oth-ers respect them and their bodies.

Why won't the female black belt on the bus endure unnecessary discomfort? Because, after years of training, it isn't who she is. It isn't part of her psychological make-up to ignore her feelings and accom-modate his. Her sense of self and self-respect empowers her to act.

The Last Resort

Okay, we're back on the bus. You've used your voice. Mr. It Takes a Long Time to Get the Hint has apologised and moved. But now, what if you bounce off the bus and are approached by balaclava-wearing, knife-wielding No 1. America's Most Wanted? He is going to rape you. You can't get away. What if you know that he is likely to become angry and want to kill you should you attempt to merely maim him? What if you have to choose between not fighting, being raped and him running away or killing him and not being raped?

Fortunately, for me at least and, generally, for other female black belts, this situation is improbable. A female black belt typi-cally doesn't take unnecessary risks—doesn't park her car in dimly lit areas, is always aware of anyone following her, doesn't leave her door unlocked, finds out who's knocking at the door before open-ing it, doesn't get off a bus in the middle of nowhere, ensures that her environment is safe. In any case, a female black belt is very unlikely to be a target of male violence. She sends out the signal, "Don't mess with me"—not appealing to a would-be attacker.

But if all precautions had been taken, and I was in this situation and had to decide . . . I'd aim to take him out. After all, I'm a fem-inist; so I'd act like one.

10
Home Is Where the Fight Is

SCOTT BEATTIE

A *breath of mist rises from the lake. There is an almost imperceptible splash as the wing of the heron skims the icy surface. As the golden morning light unfolds across the mountains, you move in deep meditation. To know the world is to know yourself and the world is intoxicating in its complexity. The cold mist on your skin enlivens your body as you practice your form.*

The blare of traffic is drowned in the chaos of the gym. Here and there students are drilling, practicing, sparring under the careful eye of their instructor. The strong smell of sweat mingles with the smells of the kitchen next door which spills into the room along with the music of the almost-tuned radio. In the midst of this pandemonium, a moment of insight, perfect as a drop of rain.

We tend to think of "space" as empty and neutral: like a box to put stuff in. But as these imaginary visions suggest, space has character: its own distinct, tangible personality. Of course it can be measured, plotted, graphed. But space is something more subjective, more human, than miles, meters, and inches. But first, let me set the scene, so to speak.

The philosophy of space has become a point of interest in recent years. Social critic and philosopher Henri Lefebvre is one of the key thinkers in the area. First published in 1976, his book, *The Production of Space* (Blackwell, 1991) remains extremely influential. Lefebvre is interested less in abstract space, and more in the conceptual maps we create of our world. More importantly, he wants to explore the role these maps play in defining society. If you have the power to make everyone see *your* map as the only reasonable and objective way of viewing the world, then you have the power – however subtle or nuanced – to shape the world.

Lefebvre was particularly worried about the ways that society uses abstract maps of space to control people. Because these maps appear to be neutral and objective, taken from the "bird's eye view," they can seem more benign than they are.

For example, one problem with the "view from space" idea of space is that we're all so small: just dots on the map. This has a flattening effect, making everyone appear the same; making conformity seem to be more widespread than it actually is. Politicians and advertisers love this approach, because it turns the diversity of human culture into a set of demographic statistics, dotted on maps and pie charts, to be sold to or governed. If Lefebvre's right, we experience the world in ways that are far from equal, but this abstract view of space smooths out the rough edges, and simplifies things. Poverty or violence, for example, look like the consequences of geographical accident, rather than design; citizens of one large geographic box are more deserving, or more civilised, than another.

Those influenced by thinkers like Lefebvre have railed against this outlook by stressing the local, the human, the intimate, the different. Against the abstract spaces of conformity (the freeway, the shopping centre, the prison) we make our *own* spaces of living. Lefevbvre calls these newly created spaces "differential spaces." They're places of resistance and individual empowerment, which erupt out of conformity and oppression.

Put another way, what we call "space" is often a "place." A place is a space that *means* something to us; a space we continually, diligently create in our everyday rituals and customs. For example, a home is much more than "a machine for living in," no matter what the modern architect Le Corbusier may think. Our home is a good example of space becoming intimate, special, humanised.

Another good example is the martial arts school—perhaps one of Lefebvre's "differential spaces." As martial artists, we experience space in many different ways, but the place in which we train, the dojo or training hall is central to the way we learn and the way we see ourselves. In fact, the dojo is, in some ways, more a "space" than our home. We do more to make it our own—to make it habitable, different, and functional.

Marking Out the Ownership of Space

As territorial creatures, human beings mark out the spaces they inhabit in different ways. Most of these tell us something about those people and the communities they build. In many dojo, Western and Eastern, you'll see hints of the activities that take place in them, and the cultural trappings that come with them. Many of these refer to the Asian roots of the art, and may include calligraphy, diagrams of pressure points, statues, paintings, trophies, portraits, news clippings, and more. These artifacts suggest traditions beyond the martial art: poetry, art, literature, philosophy, and medicine. And they appeal to more than the eyes—some schools have Asian music or incense.

Not all dojos own or have exclusive use of their own spaces, a great many rent space or share space with other groups. In these situations, you can't always customize your own space. Still, many groups have their own rituals such as placement of club banner or the portrait of the discipline's founder. These are important ways in which ties to the space are forged.

But rituals of space ownership involve more that interior design. The bow-in ceremony or the statement of a pledge demonstrate that it's more than a casual space. They show that the space belongs to *this* group at *this* time. Most groups have a ritual which must be used to leave and re-enter the dojo space such as a bow or a Chinese salute. These also serve to mark out the space as special, different from everyday life.

By defining space in this way, martial artists are saying something about themselves as a group and as individuals. Counting drills in Japanese may seem like an incidental or trivial feature: a quirk of cultural borrowing. But it's important in expressing who you are in that space. It reveals how your actions as a martial artist differ from you as a gym member or basketball player.

Rituals which show connection across space, also mark out connections across time. They not only connect practitioners to other cultures, but also to a lineage and a heritage which comes within the school. Students can perceive their place in time as inheritors of a founder (whether that founder be Asian or a local Western founder) and see their role in passing on the tradition to new generations of students.

In a Western dojo the authenticity of these rituals and ornaments varies from group to group. Some groups strive to research the best reflection of their cultural traditions while others, like notorious "nine-to-five ninjas," pick and chose from their favourite oriental clichés. Some styles reject the cultural baggage altogether and create their own local cultural accoutrements, founded in "fitness and exercise culture" or even New Age philosophy.

These rituals define the dojo, including its edges—they separate it off from other similar spaces. The dojo belongs to *this* style of Karate or Kung Fu, and this governs the kinds of techniques, forms, and philosophy which will be learnt in the space. Traditions may mark out competing schools as rivals: the Them that makes Us what we are.

By defining the space of the dojo in this way, we also contrast it to other social spaces. "Don't try this at home"—home being a space of non-violence, particularly for children who are students. Similarly, some schools talk about the difference between "street" and "dojo" techniques. The street, in this sense, is often an imaginary place from martial arts films and video games: a space of conflict and violence where the martial artist is forced to use their skills, or seek to prove themselves. Alternatively, a non-violent or non-aggressive philosophy may be enforced through the dojo's spatial rituals—a group pledge may include the vow to use skills responsibly and with respect outside of the dojo space.

Rituals of the Body

We've seen what outlines the dojo space as different. But what happens *inside?* What's the character of the space within? The rituals adopted in martial arts often focus on the development of the body, of conditioning, health, and protection of the safety of the body. Even something as simple as laying down mats in an Aikido dojo shapes the way in which space can be used and defines the possibilities of action in the space. And, of course, bodies exist in the "space" of physics: with their own mechanics, anatomy, mass and relationship to gravity.

The division of the training session into drills, forms, sparring, and other activities is something which defines the way in which a group experiences a style and its philosophy. This designates that the dojo is not a casual space in which anything goes, and that the things you do to train shapes your view of the world. A dojo that focuses on self defence will devote more time to practical exercises than one in which choreographed forms are focussed on.

These decisions have important safety aspects. By enforcing rules on safety gear, by limiting the contact between individuals to formal drills and sparring activities a focus is placed on the safety and sovereignty of the individual. Rules which prevent "fooling around" and unstructured fighting set up the dojo as a place where conflict is contained. Individuals are safe to experience it in a controlled, comfortable way, which suits their skills and confidence.

But there's more to martial arts than fighting. These body rituals go beyond sparring, and cover other aspects of well-being, like stretching before strenuous exercise, ensuring students have enough water, and looking out for any health problems. Over time the student's body is developed in strength, stamina, and fitness. But at the same time, they become more adept at monitoring and governing their own bodies. Along with this comes confidence: knowing how to move in particular ways, and what these movements mean philosophically.

Practices of Hierarchy

And part of this meaning is *knowing your place* in the space. In other words, the space of the dojo includes rituals that define the hierarchy of the school. Aspects of uniform, control, and etiquette separate the instructor from the students, and often designate hierarchies among the students. While the colored belt ranking system is a Western invention, most styles have more informal practices that do the same thing: setting apart the novices from the masters, the competent from the bungling.

Inside the dojo's walls, language also reinforces this hierarchy: commands, titles, names for objects. Indeed, the names for arms, legs, head, and left and right all change—our basic sense of orientation in space is changed to suggest the style and its tradition. We don't just "kick to the head"; we learn *mawashi geri*.

Some instructors definitely enjoy this power more than others— indeed, some insist on absurd (and sometimes fraudulent) Eastern titles. But, in general, these practices are important ways in which the dojo becomes a special place with its own set of rules and culture. Indeed, hierarchies may not just be concerned with power and control. In traditional Japanese Kendo schools, for example, the students kneel in line in order of skill and experience: the most qualified sit near the door, a ritual that harks back to when aggressors from rival schools may attack.

Uniforms are also forms of power. For example, the *dogi* – in Japanese schools – distinguishes martial arts spaces from those where clothing is a matter of convenience, or individual expression (for example a gym). And the uniform has clear hierarchical value, marking the instructor from the students, and marking students as legitimate members of the dojo. Outsiders don't get the *dogi*, or its particular patches, belts, style – everyone in the uniform is subject to the same law.

But uniforms go further than being just a tool of power. Most obviously, they express cultural tradition (like the *dogi*) and enforce a feeling of community. Indeed it can be an oddly disconcerting experience to train in ordinary clothing when you have forgotten your uniform; a strange mood of being "out of place."

Within the dojo, uniforms also heighten the focus on martial arts, rather than on wealth, or prestige, or success. They often flatten-out differences between individuals, and make it harder for wealthier students to show their status through more expensive or fashionable gym gear. This doesn't always work. I was told an anecdote about Kendo schools in Japan, where the outside of the uniforms were identical, but the wealthier students personalised the inside with expensive fabrics and stitching. And some uniforms, like those in Mixed Martial Arts, accentuate build and fitness: they stress the toned, disciplined physiques of the fighters, and uphold the hierarchy of physicality.

This might seem like a lot of disempowerment and restraint. But we're not shackled to our dojo—it's a freely-chosen, communally-created space. We accept these hierarchies because they offer new skills, experiences, and a gauge of our own progress. As opposed to a school uniform, the uniform of your dojo is a choice of lifestyle and philosophical commitment: it expresses something about yourself and your (changing) view of the world.

Philosophy of Play

The space of the dojo can encourage play. For most, the study of martial arts is a leisure activity: we are not soldiers in training but individuals for whom physical and mental development are a matter of choice, of fun. The dojo is a space structured to facilitate play.

Martial arts are concerned with conflict, a struggle between participants in which skills are tested. Of course, this can take the form of competition, which can be highly structured and organised. But this is not necessary for individuals to experience sparring as fun. As with other games, there doesn't always have to be a winner or loser, although some people are competitive by nature and want this status to be proclaimed (at least if they're the ones who win).

Despite its trivial associations, play can be a serious business. It shapes the communities we play in, and the identities we take as players. There's an important aspect of pretence in play: we discard, however briefly, our everyday identity, and explore a new one. This is very important for those who lack physical confidence, for whom the dojo can be a safe place in which to experiment. If only for a few hours, we act out the role of being a tough, fearless martial artist while supported by safety gear and rules of engagement. As Aristotle suggested long ago, virtues are best established though habits: to be brave, we have to become accustomed to acting bravely. Playing at combat in the dojo, a student's new confidence may make them less of a target for victimisation; may make them more robust, independent and fearless.

The Way of the Place

So what does this all mean? Looking into the space of the dojo reveals the crucial importance of balance. Not the perfect, dead balance of a pair of scales, but the balance of a fighter, kicking high: a moving, active, elegant harmony between opposing forces. In particular, we can see the importance of the balance of inside and outside, which is rarely still.

As martial artists we are made to be conscious of balance, between thought and emotion, between ourselves and others, between interior and exterior. The dojo is a space that has an inside, a protected environment in which to practice skills and an outside, the rest of the world in which life is not a simulation. This double life has a moral component: our duties to the school and our fellow students also suggests a duty to behave ethically in the world.

Our space rituals emphasise this balance: the way in which we shape our space, the way we leave and enter it, the uniforms we wear make us conscious of the inside and outside of the dojo. By doing this we are also aware of the fragile "skin" that separates these spaces, the layer of cloth which is our 'gi, and the permeability of the edge between spaces. A philosophy of balance is basic to all this. It's expressed through our rituals, skills, customs—they emphasise a kind of hard-won harmony, and our dependence on one another, and on fundamental laws, institutions, assumptions.

In this space, we're also conscious of our bodily balance. We realise that the relationship between ourselves and others is a fluid, changeable one; that martial arts asks questions of beauty and moral responsibility *in motion*, all tied up with how we move in space. Whether a style is graceful and artistic or brutal and pragmatic, the aesthetic values are instilled in students through drilling and forms. Does your style emphasise confrontation or deflection, hard or soft techniques, grappling or striking? In other words, how do we take up, work with, and transform our spaces?

And these spaces are social: they exist, not only between people, but between groups. In other words, the space of martial aesthetics and morality is a large one. The Chinese martial tradition includes the concept of *Jiang Hu*, or "the world of martial arts": a shared space of all martial artists, set apart from general society. It's here that the local spaces of the dojos intersect *and* define each other. They have their relative styles, values, philosophies – they compete with, and encourage, one another; they share cultural traditions, and they often criticise them. It is an ongoing, difficult, exciting balance between conflict and peace, difference and sameness, inclusion and exclusion—all centered on spaces.

While different uses and ideas of space are as varied as the world's martial artists, the space of the dojo offers a common opportunity: to express and explore who we are.

The Perfect Weapon

Ethics and Value

"I really want to kill you,
but you're not worth it"

11
Iaido, Aikido, and the Other

TAMARA KOHN

One day I came home from work to find that some prankster had, for the third day in a row, entered my back gate and knocked my rubbish bin over, spilling its decomposing messy contents all over my lawn. "That's it!" "Enough is enough!"

Something made me think the culprit or culprits could be living in one of the houses overlooking my garden from the back lane. I donned my *keiko gi* (white training uniform), *obi* (belt), and *hakama* (long black divided skirt), took out my *iaito* (training sword), and practiced *Iaido* (the art of drawing the sword) alone in my back garden for an hour, in full view of the neighbourhood during its dinner hour—drawing and striking through the air and casting the imaginary blood of my foe off my blade (*chiburi*), over and over again.

It worked. The bin was never violated again. Of course, the end to the bin tipping could have been a coincidence, but the need I felt to release my frustration through training, my hope that someone responsible would see me and think twice about carrying on, and my imagination about the absent Other which provided the target for my sword and whose aggression drew the perfect response, all contributed to a tremendous sense of achievement (at the time)!

In my head, the absent Other came bounding into my back garden to spar with me and was defeated—peacefully (insofar as no real blood was shed). Attending to the Other—even one without a name, face, or history—is what being human is all about, and martial training is a perfect playing field for such a discovery, because it's a place where such attendance can mean the difference between life and death (at least in theory).

Action, reaction, and reflection at any time will hinge on attending to others, whether they are in your face or in your thoughts. Yet there are many ways to consider others, some more considerate, others more selfish. Here are some questions:

- **How important is the physical presence of the Other to our understanding of ourselves?**

- **Is the "in-your-face-ness" of the Other just as important, or even more important, than the "in-your-head-ness" of the Other?**

- **Is reacting to an Other's face-to-face punch to your nose going to affect your sense of who you are in the wider world in the same way as sitting alone in a dojo with a sword, slicing the imaginary enemy's block off?**

- **Is looking after the (real or virtual) Other as important or more important than looking after oneself?**

There isn't a straight answer to any of these. Western Philosophers have been arguing over this relationship between the self and others for several centuries—maybe they just needed the right (martial arts) experience to find the right set of clues . . . (*Mr Green . . .* in the *dojo. . . .* with the *sword?*).

The Drawing of the Sword

Many martial arts include solitary practice of set forms or *kata* that have been developed in order to strengthen and train the body through repetition to the point where your body moves reactively—without thinking. Iaido is a solitary practice of the Japanese art of "drawing the sword," and it involves engaging (as in my back yard) with an imaginary Other as we work through a repertoire of forms. The word *Iaido* can be translated as "the way of mental presence and immediate action," or "the way of harmonizing oneself in action." In this practice there's no sparring, no "Who draws fastest wins!", no "My sword's sharper than your sword!" The imaginary Other, virtually decapitated and disemboweled thousands of times, walks away unscathed while the sword-wielder sharpens his or her mind and body through practice and more practice in trying to achieve that ever-elusive perfect cut.

The virtual Other can be seen as a tool here—an imaginary means to an end—a target one must pass through and beyond. The timing of the draw and the skill of the cut depend on having an intimate connection to the imagined attack, but it's still all in the head. So when training alone, my obligation is to myself—*my* mental presence, *my* action, even if there might be moments of polite consideration built into the forms that I practice. (Like my favourite beheading technique, *dakikubi*, where the drawing of the sword and standing at readiness before striking to aid in the Other's *seppuku*—ritual suicide—must be done in total silence, so the pre-death stillness of the poor virtual bugger who is about to lose his or her virtual life and head will not be disturbed.) Most movements in *Iaido kata* aren't about looking after Others, but about preserving one's self through efficient, clean, precise (and deadly) movements that the self controls.

Hmmmm. As a martial artist and a humanist, I wonder about this self-ish framing of any practice. I like to think I care about others—all the time; that I don't just use others to get what I want. Something bothers me about my own response in my own backyard to Mr. Rubbish Tipper. (I only imagine it must have been a man, but that's beside the point.)

I'm disturbed by my memory of my response because in most martial training I've encountered, the Other is not just imagined but is a real energy-wielding person, and my relation to him or her is necessarily very attentive and engaged. In Aikido, a Japanese martial art I adore and have practiced for many years, the others I train with (known friends and unknown strangers) all have real faces and bodies. I have to look after my partners because, at the very least, I want to train with them again tomorrow and next week. But there are deeper reasons to look after them in my training, and these relate to a more general ethic of care, something philosophers have talked about in all sorts of contexts—not surprisingly, often with reference to situations of conflict. (For our purposes, these could be seen as the raw material of martial training.)

The Art of Peace and Love . . .

Aikido is an entirely defensive practice—though in reality, you can't practice alone: defense is only possible when a real committed attack has been launched (as opposed to a virtual imagined attack). The moment the energy of an attack moves towards you in Aikido, then movement (entering or turning) becomes possible—the energy of the throw or pin that a proficient aikidoka produces from that attack does not come out of his or her own strength—it's taken out of the momentum and power from the Other—it draws the attacker into contact, and redirects the Other's movement to a point where balance is lost.

It's helpful to look at the characters that make up the name of the art—*ai* (harmonizing—a term that implies interaction with an Other), *ki* (energy in its largest sense) and *do* ("way" or path; in

Chinese, "Dao"). This defensive practice, with its sole aim to harmonize with and then neutralize the energy of an attack, is never solitary—the "Path" that the individual aikidoka traverses is built from the endless training that is conducted with others. But are these others, like the imagined Iaido others, just tools for practicing, for honing one's own skills, for sharpening one's own techniques; or are they intrinsically more important than that?

It's really quite ironic, in a way, that I should find myself reflecting about the importance of the Other in training when so much of the conversation within the martial arts dwells on the self or practitioner as the all-important subject (treading one's own path, improving oneself, polishing one's own spirit, and so on), and often ignores the Other as receiver or object. The founder of Aikido, Morihei Ueshiba, wrote that Aikido is the "art of knowing oneself." I recently published an article entitled "Creatively Sculpting the Self through the Discipline of Martial Arts Training" (in *Exploring Regimes of Discipline: Ethnographic and Analytical Inquiries*, edited by N. Dyck, Berg, 2008). Not long ago, Marlene in the dojo's changing room said that Aikido is key to her "personal development." Me, me, me.

"So what *is* so important about the Other?!" you might ask, particularly if you too are into the martial arts and have entered that world because of what it could offer *you* (self-realization, tight abs and thighs, a door to Japanese or other cultures, a confident walk in dark alleys, a job as a stunt-person, a better sense of balance, a way to deal with an abusive boss). Here are a couple of answers why we should care about the Other, and why this caring—while not the first thing that necessarily comes to our minds—may somehow be more primary to martial-arts training than the self-oriented transforming or educational benefits that makes it so attractive:

- You *are* the Other when you are receiving a technique in any paired practice, so you can't get away from it anyway (*ukemi* or the art of receiving or falling is in many ways harder to master than the techniques themselves and offers quite a lot, as you know if you've been so sore from receiving techniques for hours at an Aikido camp that your bum muscles won't let you walk up stairs). Being the Other in a martial context allows for a great deal of freedom in the encounter. I need to act to protect my body when it's been thrown (to be flexible, connected, to roll and recover . . .) and I then *choose* to run like the dickens out of the dojo (fairly unusual selection) or to return to attack again.

• What swings round comes round. This, of course, relates to number one: If, in applying your technique, you bash your partner into the ground with a force that he or she is not able to receive safely, then you will likely lose popularity on the mat (people will avoid training with you or indeed run out the door) or you may find that when it's your turn for *ukemi*, gentle "loving kindness" will not be running through your partner's mind when gauging how hard or far to throw you.

Enter Some Philosophers

Let's think about this one for a bit more. Reciprocity is built into training, as it is in all social activity. The notion that we have responsibility for our actions is supported by the idea that whatever happens in our encounters with other people, there is the possibility of reciprocity. So it's good to dish out what you want on your own plate. Most would agree with that. Not that *all* people in the world (ax-murderers? thieves? bin dumpers?) always dish out what they want to receive on their own plates, of course, but let's agree at least on the general principle. This is what musing about "ethics" is all about—coming up with a principle that can, perhaps, be shared.

The twentieth-century philosopher, Emmanuel Levinas, had a great interest in ethics and the responsibilities that individuals have to other people in their world. When selves and others meet up (in training, at work, at home, on the street) at any given moment there will be what Levinas calls an "uneven mutuality" in the encounter. He wrote, "I am responsible for the Other without waiting for reciprocity, were I to die for it. Reciprocity is *his* affair" (*Totality and Infinity*, Martinus Nijhoff, 1961; p. 98). If this is true, then the promise of reciprocity is *not* what initially motivates you and me to act responsibly and with care, even if it is part of the equation overall – just being with others is what does it.

So if you think about the Aikido encounter on the mat, this responsibility you have to the Other happens before you touch— before the Other's attacking energy moves your body into a response. It floats in the air around you and in the books you've read and sermons you've heard and the mothering you've received;

it's reinforced in the dojo instructions posted in changing rooms, it's been drilled into good Christians ("love thy neighbour") and Zen Buddhists who wouldn't squash a fly. Doshu Ueshiba Moriteru (the grandson of the founder of aikido, Morehei Ueshiba, and the current leader of the Aikido World Headquarters in Japan) wrote as part of his New Year's message this year—Aikido's answer to the Queen's Speech—

> It is important to be harmonious in Aikido. Part of being in harmony is to observe and accept people as they are. To find harmony one must be accepting, giving, and correcting with a feeling of kindness. In Aikido both partners play the role of being uke and nage. In this there is an opportunity to feel compassion for the other person, this in turn allows your spirit to grow. Through training with one another we develop our respect and appreciation for each other. . . . We must learn to treasure one another . . .
> (www13.big.or.jp/~aikikai/e_new.html)

Yes, treasuring is good. We learn to treasure, but we also *choose* to treasure others for all the reasons that we've seen, and more. I almost always treasure and respect my Aikido partners. I can't say that for my bin-tipping faceless coward(s) in the lane. Levinas says that when you're confronted by "the face" of the Other you become open to its vulnerability and are immediately and infinitely responsible. How you act with that individual then goes beyond courtesy and politeness, and this extends far beyond the martial arts to our face-to-face encounters with all others. This bigger idea is that we all share in our humanity and universal responsibility (as opposed to the "It's not my problem so why should I care?" attitude). It's therefore fitting that instead of defining philosophy as the "Love of Wisdom," Levinas called it "The Wisdom of Love."

Hannah Arendt in her reflections on post-war German guilt further extends this issue of responsibility, and has written that "the idea of humanity, when purged of all sentimentality, has the very serious consequence that in one form or another men must assume responsibility for all crimes committed by men" (*The Portable Hannah Arendt,* Penguin, 2003; pp.154-155). Shame or guilt is an expression of this responsibility. So . . . taking on conflict in a responsibly martial way is an act of accepting and honestly reacting to neutralize any conflict in any context. To engage in self-defense is to engage in a world where self-defense is necessary—or at least possible. We learn to defend against a possibility that *we ourselves have created through being responsible*—Arendt would urge us to feel that we all are accountable for the conflict from others that is out there. And it is out there. Dead of night bin-tippers round every turn. Explosive devices in every shoe. Drunken louts in respectable venues.

Touch

Which brings me to another reason why attention to the Other is important: Touch and Intimacy. A hazy memory takes me back now to a delicious meal at a Balti Indian restaurant in Birmingham, England. It was near the end of an Aikido seminar, and many participants attended the dinner. I know I drank way too much. I burned myself on the sizzling Balti dish handles trying to lift the bloody thing with my "ki" (which unfortunately left little welts on my wrists that I still wear today!). At some point I approached the most senior British Aikido sensei there—a terribly shy and gentle man off the mat and a powerful confident presence on the mat. I asked him what drew him into Aikido in the first place. "It allows me to touch many other people and be physically close to them every day without threat." My internal reaction: "Whoa, no way!" and "Yeah, me too!"—all at the same time.

His was a wonderful response that was entirely honest, in total keeping with Aikido philosophy, but also said in a way that most martial arts publications I've seen would probably hesitate to reveal. To say "I love Aikido because of all the physical touching and intimacy with strangers" is surely a bit creepy to someone who wouldn't quite understand the special contact that defines such paired practice. Actually, you probably wouldn't really ponder the question of your touchy-feely motives during the training itself— you wouldn't have time! In all Budo training, there's meant to be no time to ponder anything. "You think too much!" is a frequent refrain from my master teacher. He can see people thinking in the tiniest hesitations of movement and timing of his students' reactions when they are mentally reasoning instead of reacting bodily (paradoxically the latter is often called a "natural" response, but it only comes after years of repetitive training).

Anyway, it's fair to say that on the mat, others in paired training are not a faceless threat but a necessary and intimate and desired force that offer themselves to you, and that draw you into a response. Later on, warmed up with beer and curry, you can wax lyrical about the meanings and attractions of that on-the-mat intimacy with others in the "know": the joy of a fine sweaty neck lock (not if yours is the head in the armpit, however), the pleasure of a well timed hip throw, or the special contact from a good training partner that makes everything you do feel magical.

I Kant Get Enough of Your Love . . . or Kan I?

In an art where the emphasis is to blend, neutralize and escape, rather than to fight, overpower and win, the idea of the self is given up in the interest of the Other. At least this is true in theory, especially as far as interest in "winning" and "losing" is concerned; but let's face it, one can still be selfish in training without spoiling for a fight or wanting a trophy. I'm selfish when I avoid BamBam on the mat because (as the nickname might indicate) he lacks sensitivity; I'm selfish when I don't teach *suwariwaza* (techniques on

the knees) on a day when I've had my toenails painted; I'm selfish when I skip class because a teacher I don't really like has replaced the one I do. Which all raises the question: What motivates my actions, and can I be selflessly focussed on the Other and selfishly focused on myself at the same time? This is connected with the earlier question about the relationship between selves and others when they stand face-to-face vs. when they never meet at all.

The non-competitive nature of Aikido draws many people in to train in the first place—many hobble over with their knee injuries from Judo and Karatedo to practice a very powerful art that they find is kinder on their joints because of the different emphasis. So (selfish?) self-preservation motivates the move on the one hand, but the grander philosophy of selflessness and protection of others has also prompted the shift. I don't have any problem with the idea that I act to protect myself and care for myself *and* look after my partner or attacker all at the same moment. But which comes first: the care and protection of the self or the responsibility to the Other? Can one say that one of those obligations is greater in value or importance than the other one?

Well, we know Levinas and Arendt are two who would bat for the responsibility-for-the-Other team. They would insist that in the realm of ethics, caring for others matters more than caring for oneself. Levinas would have qualified this to add that it is out of the face-to-face encounter with the Other that this ethic of care arises and that this comes first—it's pre-cultural, pre-experience—it's just plain human. Morals, he would have added, however, are different beasts—they are culturally laden and situational—attached to events, places and times.

Back in the eighteenth century, the German philosopher Immanuel Kant also tried to demonstrate in his *Groundwork for a Metaphysics of Morals*, how our actions emerge out of our self-love and desire to protect our selves *as well as* a need to look after others. They are both important but different. Kant argued that caring for other humans *and* oneself is always essential—it's what he called a "categorical imperative," as opposed to a "hypothetical imperative" that depends on the situation. This is a bit like Levinas's distinction between ethics and morals. The first is taken to be generalizable—it intends to work in all places and times (Look after others and don't kill them . . . ever! Even in your head!), while the second is associated with opinion and culture (Thou shalt not sleep with thy sensei's wife . . . unless thou happen to live in a polygamous society where that's deemed okay!). This all starts to make sense in my mind when I return back to the lawn, the sword, and the garbage bins, and reflect on what made me act as I did back then.

Back at the Bins, or Loving Your Enemy Like Your Neighbor

Was it the right response to my bin-tipping "enemy" to practice my sword drawing and cutting in my back yard? I could say it worked for me at the time, but that's an *entirely* selfish response. I should tell you something that happened after the incident. I got a letter from a neighbor in the cul-de-sac. He hadn't seen my dramatic display of Iaido prowess. And he *said* he had no knowledge of who tipped the bins into my garden. However, he had learned about the problem and wanted me to know that he and others in the lane really resented the fact that my "ugly bins" at the back of my property faced the fronts of their beautiful homes and sullied the view. He asked if I could move them. I did (to the front of my property where they could sully the view of less fussy neighbors).

So where does this leave us? If Hannah Arendt was right, and I suspect she was, then I find that I become responsible for the problem that I set out to solve with my sword, and my reflective concern about my behavior that night is evidence of this. The violence of the bin-tipping was maybe, at least in part, due to my own actions. Actions *do* hinge upon one's understanding of the Other and the Other's presence or not.

My reaction, my violent slicing and dicing of Mr Faceless Absent Man in my Iaido gear was a doubly self-centered display (first in terms of wanting to be seen by neighbors and secondly in terms of wanting to practice with my sword). If I had taken the responsibility heeding the call to care for my attacker, I wouldn't have gone out into the garden at all (unless it was to put out the garbage). The offense started much earlier than I had imagined with my ugly bins ruffling my neighbors' feathers (obviously our moral, aesthetic, and neighborly senses didn't match) and so I ended up hacking an imagined Other's body into wee pieces and wiping the blade.

I treated this imagined Other's body as a means to an end—an *object* of hate—rather than a *subject* of love or an end in itself. Following Levinas, it all might have been different had I met "the Face" of my attacker from the start! Of course it would have! I would have responded using both principles of Aikido movement and principles guided by the Wisdom of Love. I would have stepped off line, and redirected his attack with the sweetest possible apology and maybe a life-affirming hug.

12
Epistemic Viciousness in the Martial Arts

GILLIAN RUSSELL

When I was eleven, my form teacher, Mr. Howard, showed some of my class how to punch. We were waiting for everyone else to finish changing after gym, and he took a stance that I would now call *shizentai yoi* and snapped his right fist forward into a head-level straight punch, pulling his left back to his side at the same time. Then he punched with his left, pulling back on his right. We all lined up in our ties and sensible shoes (this was England) and copied him—left, right, left, right. Afterwards he told us that if we practiced in the air really hard for three years, then we would be able to use our fists to kill a bull with one blow.

I worshipped Mr. Howard (though I would sooner have died than told him that) and so, as a skinny, eleven-year-old girl, I came to believe that if I practiced enough, I would be able to kill a bull with one blow by the time I was fourteen. I'm going to talk about epistemic viciousness in the martial arts, and this story is an illustration of just that. *Epistemic* means having to do with beliefs and their justification. *Viciousness* normally suggests deliberate cruelty and violence; but I use it here with its more old-fashioned meaning: *possessing of vices*. (The opposite being a *virtue*.) Vices (such as avarice, alcoholism and nail-biting) are ordinary things, and most of us struggle with a few, but *epistemic* vices are defects with respect to the formation of beliefs. My eleven-year-old self possessed the epistemic vice of *gullibility*, which lead me to form the false belief about killing bulls.

Other epistemic vices—such as closed-mindedness—can also lead to us *not* forming true beliefs when we ought to. Consider the internet-surfing Karate-sensei who stumbles upon an article claiming that chocolate milk is better than water or sports drinks for promoting recovery after exercise, and describing an experiment using stationary bikes performed at the University of Indiana, purporting to support this claim. Surfng Sensei is a skeptical guy; he is aware that the fitness industry is fuelled by fads and lies and he long ago developed a vocal blusteriness in response to fitness advice: it's all nonsense designed to make money. He often bangs on about this to his students: all this stuff about protein-shakes and proper form and recovery and what-not is stupid. If you want to get better at running, you've got to run more, and if you get thirsty when you're cycling on a stationary bike, drink water; nothing will make you better at cycling—except more cycling. So Surfer Sensei doesn't even consider the results of the experiment at the University of Indiana. The corruption of the fitness industry has driven him towards the vice of closed-mindedness; he has a tendency to ignore certain kinds of evidence which could lead an epistemically virtuous agent to form a new belief.

Karateka, and practitioners of the Japanese *gendai budo* (modern martial ways) in general, like to extol the virtues of character that training in a martial art promotes. Yet whatever the moral virtues of the well-trained budoka, the culture of training in many martial arts actually *promotes* epistemic vice, including both closed-mindedness and gullibility, but also unwarranted epistemic deference to seniors and historical sources, lack of curiosity about important related disciplines, and lack of intellectual independence. This makes them unreliable when it comes to forming beliefs.

Beliefs in the Martial Arts

What kinds of beliefs am I talking about here? I'm mostly interested in the *martial* parts of the martial arts—the teachings that pertain to fighting and self-defense, as opposed to those that pertain to competing in a sporting tournament, or how one ought to live one's life. Some of these beliefs are about particular techniques, such as (and I make no claim here about whether these examples are true):

- **that your opponent's roundhouse kicks are more dangerous whilst you are closing on him or her, than they are once you've closed**

- **that when fish-hooking the mouth, it is important to avoid being bitten**

And some beliefs will be about the interaction between certain techniques and the strategic situation more generally:

- **that slapping the ground with your arm when falling is more risky when you are on uneven ground than it is when you are on nicely sprung tatami**

- **that kicks to the head are easier and less of an invitation to a tackle when your opponent is situated downhill (or downstairs) from you**

And then there will also be beliefs about related topics, such as training, physical fitness, anatomy, fight-psychology and history:

- **that at the beginning of a fight you'll burn though all your blood sugar and can expect to feel exhausted**

- **that Anko Itosu was never in a fight, but Miyamoto Musashi and Choki Motobu liked to get in six before breakfast**

Learning a martial art is not *merely* a matter of acquiring beliefs, of course. We learn skills, gain balance and strength, develop muscle memory and proprioceptive abilities, and learn reactions and instincts for timing that can even be tricky to put into words. But, for some reason, people are particularly likely to acquire *crazy* beliefs in the martial arts. We've all heard the stories about martial artists who believe they can use their *chi* to kill someone without touching them, and read YouTube comments from kids who think that ninja nerve-strikes are banned in the UFC on the grounds that they are "too deadly." (A glance at the UFC rules will debunk that one.) Harry Cook's multipart articles on the concept of *ki* in *Classical Fighting Arts* are a chronicle of budo gullibility, and include the horrifying story of a seventeen-year-old boy who attempted to stop a train by taking up a kung fu stance in its path.

But it's not just lunatics and kids who pick up odd beliefs. Just last week I was on the way home from a Judo class with a friend—a senior judoka and university student—who insisted that although there was nothing wrong with lifting weights, strength was unimportant in judo, and it wouldn't help one to become a better Judo player. The appropriate reply is, of course, unprintable. My friend has seen plenty of examples of the value of strength in Judo, has done hours of strength-conditioning in a Judo dojo where they've installed a weights room upstairs, and despite copious experiential data in support of the contrary hypothesis (the kind of data that can read off three-minute *newaza* (groundwork) sessions with someone fifty pounds heavier than yourself) he still somehow believed it when he was told that strength isn't at all important in Judo.

Judo is an art in which there is relatively little room for pretence; in *randori* (free practice) either you manage to throw your opponent, or you don't. In *newaza* either you escape from your opponent's hold or you don't. So if a belief in the unimportance of strength manages to survive the training that Judo offers, it isn't surprising that it thrives in arts, such as Aikido, where there is usually less competitive *randori*, and more *yakusoku kumite* (pre-arranged sparring). One particularly bizarre story from my own experience involves a young male karateka whose natural physical makeup and Judo training had made him unusually strong. Really, *unusually* strong—this is the only time I have heard of a Karate club having to buy thicker *makiwara* because a *beginner* was routinely snapping them by accident. But after a few years away, the man began training with a local branch of the Ki Society, who denigrated the importance of his strength. He eventually returned to us stripped of much of his muscle-mass, convinced that there was a kind of disreputable immorality associated with physical strength, and that the main way he could improve his martial ability was to let his muscles atrophy and develop his *ki*.

His teachers were, I think, fantasists, but I want to know why are there so many fantasists in the martial arts, as compared to other activities. You won't find many sprinters or removal-men who will tell you that strength doesn't matter to their chosen tasks; nor will you find power-lifters who think they can move the bar without touching it or high-ranking engineers who specialize in *ki*-distribution.

On Going to the Dojo Like You're Going to Church

A piece of the puzzle is that a lot of people treat their martial art as sacred. Not just special, and important and worthwhile—like, say, a vocation—but like a religion. Their sensei is basically the agent of the Founders on Earth, infallible on all matters martial, and the writings of the founder are treated as the word of god. Members feel guilty if they don't go, and risk being regarded as morally deficient if they leave. Minor infractions of the social and dress codes are also moralized (having red toe-nails in the dojo is like going to church in a mini-skirt and halter-top—you can do it, but it's no way to get into the choir) and the students of other martial arts are talked about as if they're practicing the wrong religion.

In religion, people seek something that will satisfy their desire for the special, mysterious, and meaningful in their lives, which is exactly what some of us hope to find in the martial arts. But though this means that the sanctification of the dojo isn't particularly surprising, it also provides a clue as to how some of the wackier beliefs find fertile ground there: people who are hungry for something special—and that's all of us to some degree—are more likely to be suckers, because strong desires make people vulnerable. If you're very hungry, you might search all your life and die disappointed, or you might eventually give in and satisfy the desire by lowering your epistemic standards, so that you come to believe— falsely—that you've found something that exotic already.

The tendency to treat your martial art as sacred also seems to encourage a style of thinking according to which the art and the teachers aren't merely good, but are the best anything or anyone can possibly be—in any respect one can think of. Some people end up believing, for example, that Karate is not merely a good workout, but *the best possible physical exercise ever.* I came across an example of this in the *Journal of Asian Martial Arts* a few years ago. I don't mean to pick on the writer as an exceptionally bad case, just a convenient one who happened to express the ideas in a prominent place. The writer, reviewing a book on Yoga for martial artists, began by writing:

> It is difficult for this reader to understand why anyone who is practicing karate would ever need or want to practice yoga to help their karate. *Is something lacking in the study and practice of karate that warrants turning to another form of exercise to accomplish karate's goals?* It is highly doubtful to this reader. . . .

Oh, come on! Karate, practiced in isolation, tends to overdevelop the lateral quadriceps compared to the vastus medialis and adductors, making the patella of many karateka a bit frog-eyed. All that punching over-develops the chest, anterior deltoids and triceps with respect to the back, posterior deltoids and biceps, contributing to poor posture and a tight chest. Unbalanced leg muscles and sweeps are a nasty combination, and so are insufficient development of the rotator cuff and repeatedly having to receive *ikkyo* (a technique that involves manipulating your opponent's body by manipulating their arm), and if you are practicing Karate seriously, it's better that you should know all this.

Admittedly, I am assuming that getting injured—especially things like knee and shoulder injuries that often linger on for years—is no way to accomplish Karate's goals. But if you'll grant me that, then what we have is a reason to add something to Karate from the outside, by giving new karateka a gentle push in the direction of the power-rack and the pull-up bar. I take my claims here to be unexceptional, though no doubt they'll offend the True Believers. But right or wrong, it won't be possible to dispute these points reasonably by assuming that karateness is next to godliness, and ignoring anything that comes into conflict with that.

Rei unto Sensei

The Problem with Investment

Not everyone treats their martial art like a religion; but another, more inevitable, problem is that those who already have beliefs in the area tend to have a lot invested in those beliefs, and the people whose testimony we are most likely to trust have inevitably invested *years* of effort.

Suppose that Kenji has been studying Shotokan Karate for twenty years. He had a lot of trouble with a particular style of side-kick early on, finding it hard to make his knee do what his teacher's knee did, but one day his elderly teacher took him aside and showed him how using his hip-flexor and obliques in a slightly different way made the kick much easier to perform. Kenji was impressed and since then he has been able to execute a kick which closely resembles that of his teacher. Kenji eventually ended up teaching Karate, and whenever he has a student who struggles with the kick in question, he takes them aside and teaches them his teacher's trick, feeling proud that he is able to pass on this information, and contribute to his students' progress. Very occasionally a new student will ask him what the kick is useful for, and, like his teacher before him, he tells them that it is used in competition, but that its *real* use is in disarming an attacker by kicking the knife from their hands. Kenji subscribes to the following belief: this particular side-kick is an important and effective Karate technique. He has a lot invested in this belief, and it would be painful to give it up: he struggled for years to master the technique, and if it is not a useful technique, all that will have been wasted. He taught the technique to many students; if he comes to believe that it is not an effective technique, he would have to admit that he had mislead them, and that would be very embarrassing.

Down the pub one night, a lot of evidence is presented to Kenji that goes against his belief: friend A, a physiotherapist, observes the kick and tells Kenji that the technique will be detrimental to the stability of his and his students' knees. Friend B, a professional cage-fighter, argues that the technique is useless and points out that no-one has ever used it in a full-contact fight, and that's because you can't get any useful force behind it (except against your own ligaments). Friend C, a historian of the martial arts, argues that the kick is not to be found in any of the precursors of the Shotokan Kata. It is, he argues, a late addition to the style that probably crept in by mistake. Finally Friend D, an expert in knife-fighting, tells Kenji that the disarming technique simply wouldn't work in general, and that he has underestimated the danger of closing on a blade, and the lengths that good knife-fighters instinctively go to to protect their blade-hands. Typically, he says, a fighter would have little trouble blocking the kick with the other arm or a leg, and would then immediately counter with the knife.

That's a lot of evidence and expert testimony to crop up in one night, but Kenji *really* doesn't want to give up his belief that the kick is a good technique. He gets in a horrible argument with his friends at the pub, but on the way home on his own realizes that it's actually easy to maintain his belief in the effectiveness of the kick. First, he should have told A that health is one thing, and martial ability is another; perhaps training in Karate will get you a few injuries over the years, but we're not training for health, but to be able to fight. Then he should have told B that cage-fighting is stupid and immoral (so there), and obviously doesn't involve knives. Friend C is a smart guy and so he should have expressed interest in his historical findings, but pointed out first, that it is not always easy for an outsider to interpret kata, and then he should have said that Karate is a living art and it's natural that when new techniques are discovered, they are added to the curriculum. The Boston Crab wasn't originally a part of Judo, but that doesn't mean that it's not an effective Judo technique. Finally, for Friend D, who claimed that the disarming technique wouldn't work, he plans the response: you just aren't doing it right. Our kick is difficult and takes many years to perfect—no-one said the martial arts were easy. If you train in it long enough, it will work.

None of these answers is really sufficient, and some of them are outright irrelevant, but Kenji isn't trying to convince his friends, but simply maintain his own mental coherence whilst retaining the belief in which he has invested so deeply. It is hard to imagine someone *without Kenji's level of investment*—say his brother Tenji—maintaining the belief in the face of such evidence. Suppose Tenji has taken on the ambitious project of constructing a martial art from scratch and so far he has never so much as spent a minute practicing or teaching any techniques, he just wants to design the most effective martial art possible. Tenji hears about a new throw, and is considering adding it, but then is told by experts that the throw is dangerous for the lower back of the person performing it, wouldn't work in a sport fight, isn't a traditional martial arts technique, but something that was invented yesterday by the guy down the road; and finally that the throw isn't a technique which should be used martially, because it involves allowing your opponent into your *shikaku* (dead angle) which is too risky. It's absurd to think that Tenji would talk himself out of accepting all these points and add the technique to his new art. Why would he? *He* doesn't have any reason to.

Trust Me, I'm Your Sensei

The trouble is that when you're just starting out, you don't have much choice. A martial art can't be learned from a book; you have to learn from someone who already knows what they're doing, and so, depending a little on where you live, if you find a single club in a single art which has an experienced teacher and lots of adult senior students who look strong, and can do stuff that you'd like to be able to do, then that club might well be your *only* decent bet for learning about the martial arts.

Deference to one's teacher is both traditional and expected in many training environments; but without a common background of Confucianism to ground such deference, contemporary dojo interpret the idea in many different ways. Some clubs are run like military boot camps (Drop and give me twenty maggot! Yes, sir! Bow to your sensei! Yes, sir!); some like an extended family in which rank is *never* pulled, because it would be beneath the dignity of those who have rank to bother; and some clubs seem like a secret society where you never quite know where you stand or what the rules are (Is sensei not criticizing my footwork any longer because I've got it right now, or is it because he's given up on me? I wonder whether it's okay to ask? Maybe he'd be annoyed and give up on me. . . .)

Regardless of the cultural norms in your dojo, and whatever was expected in traditional China, Okinawa, or Japan, it does seem that respect—respect beyond the normal respect accorded to every human being—is something that is appropriate for anyone who knows a lot about the martial arts and who is sincerely trying to teach you some of what he or she knows. So how do you maintain that respect whilst remaining epistemologically vice-free? If your sensei says something that you think is obviously false ("you can't kick me from there"), it doesn't seem all that respectful to answer "sure I can, look! . . . there!"

Respect for your sensei can require you not to challenge every apparent falsehood you hear from his or her lips. However, there's a lot of distance between that and believing everything that they say. The epistemically virtuous are cautious in what they *believe*, but that won't normally get in the way of decent behavior. You can show respect by keeping quiet when it's appropriate, and, within your own mind, you can show respect to someone by giving serious weight to the fact that *they* have made a claim. When your five-year-old cousin says "You can't kick me from there, asshole", you might smile and walk by secure in the belief that he's wrong, but when someone you respect as your teacher says it, and it *still* seems obviously false, respect demands that you try to resolve the tension. Depending on the personality of your sensei, you might be able to ask them about it and get a serious answer—even if you have to wait until you get them alone. Maybe you'll find it convincing, maybe not—and if not there's no need to go on and on about it—but either way you've taken both your teacher, and your own commitment to the truth, seriously. This is the best-case scenario. Maybe the atmosphere in your dojo is more formal than this, or your sensei is a bit touchier about being challenged. In that case you might need to approach a senior student or try to work it out for yourself. Again, you might be able to, or you might decide that he was really just wrong about this. But either way, no genuine requirement of deference to your sensei can require that you believe something false or unjustified, just as no genuine requirement of deference to your sensei could require that you do something morally wrong if they asked you to.

Deferring to History

Just as there is a tendency to defer to seniority in the martial arts, so there is a tendency to defer to history. When a budoka says "Kentsu Yabu said you should practice your kata thirty times a day," there is a good chance that they aren't just relating an interesting historical fact; they are actually *telling you* to practice your kata thirty times a day.

Such an inference—Famous Historical Master said such and such, therefore you should believe such and such—doesn't pass muster in other areas. Try telling a long-distance runner that Pheidippides (the original marathoner) said that athletes should not spend time thinking about their equipment, but should focus their minds on the gods. They might say something like "Oh yes, that's interesting"; but they *wouldn't* infer that they should stop replacing their running shoes every four hundred miles. Runners think that the contemporary staff of *Runner's World* know more about running than all the ancient Greeks put together.

It's not just other physical activities where history is kept in its place; the same is true in any well-developed area of study. It's not considered disrespectful for a physicist to say that Isaac Newton's theories are false. Newton is a giant among physicists, but since physics is a serious endeavor, epistemic deference to historical figures is not required, and the fact that Newton, or Einstein, or Aristotle, believed that such and such is not regarded as a reason to believe that such and such. (It's probably worth noting that amongst crank physicists the authority of certain dashing figures—especially Einstein, Bohr, Feynman, and Hawking—is given more weight, and they may write as if the "Hawking thinks such and such, therefore such and such" inference is likely to go through, just as I occasionally meet people at parties who think "Chuck Norris thinks such and such, therefore such and such" is a persuasive argument in the martial arts.)

Ow! But Chuck Norris said it would work!

But forget Chuck Norris, and consider Miyamoto Musashi and Takuan Soho, Gichin Funakoshi and Kenwa Mabuni, Jigoro Kano and Kyuzo Mifune, Morihei Ueshiba and Takeda Sokaku, Yim Wing Chun and Sun Tzu. In the martial arts—even in the *gendai budo*, which aren't all that old—founders, ancient writers, traditions and historical masters are treated with such epistemic deference that their sayings often go unquestioned even when they conflict with each other, with common sense, with contemporary science, and with other important sources of information—such as one's eyes.

I am not suggesting that the founders and practitioners who went before you do not deserve respect. But again, respect never requires inappropriate moral *or epistemic* deference. I'm enormously fond of the writings of Gichin Funakoshi; in a discipline where many practitioners are neither gentle nor modest, *Karate-do: My Way of Life* is an extraordinarily gentle and modest autobiography. But despite Funakoshi's stature in Karate, and my admiration for him, it would be daft for me to believe everything he says, because he says some things that are daft. For example, he writes that Karate can cure any illness except for physical injuries, and:

> If a man who runs a temperature practices karate until the sweat begins to pour from his body, he will soon find that his temperature has dropped to normal, and that his illness has been cured.

Fever is a symptom of diverse medical conditions, including influenza, smallpox, HIV, lupus, and the common cold. Not all of these fevers can be cured by doing karate. This is why, when your six-year-old wakes up with a temperature of 104°F, you call the doctor instead of handing her the kongoken. Funakoshi's error is entirely excusable if his access to this kind of medical knowledge was restricted—but I could not be similarly excused if I believed him, and acted on that belief-now.

Poverty and Vice

How did we get to be so vicious in the martial arts? Why aren't people sanctifying the shot-put and turning their wasted, marathoning backs on Amby Burfoot when his advice is contradicted by the Ancient Greeks? Another part of the puzzle is that we martial artists struggle with a kind of poverty—data-poverty—which makes our beliefs hard to test.

Learning about some subjects, such as human anatomy, is straight-forward: get hold of a copy of the latest edition of Netter's *Anatomy*, and start reading. If you want to know more, or you become skeptical of the information presented, you can visit a lab and observe or take part in the dissection of cadavers. Like those who have gone before you, you can get out a scalpel and check for yourself.

But you can't learn Karate or White Crane Boxing from a book, and there are a lot of martial beliefs that we don't get to *test* in such a direct way. You can't *check* to see how much force, and exactly which angle a neck-break requires, or learn from experience about the psychological effects and stopping power of an eye-gouge—at least, you can't unless you're unfortunate enough to be fighting a hand-to-hand war.

In an epistemically ideal—though morally horrible—situation, we'd be able to test the effectiveness of techniques by doing them in realistic set-ups over and over again. How many times out of one hundred does your no-holds barred *nukite* to the throat result in death within five minutes? Ten, twenty, eighty, one hundred? What's the most likely alternative outcome? Bruising? Scratching? Coughing? Unconsciousness? Internal bleeding? Partially crushed trachea? Escalation? Can subjects partially armor against it or roll with it? These questions have answers, but for good ethical reasons, we can't get at them by direct testing; and though martial techniques do get used "for real", this rarely happens as part of a controlled experiment.

Our inability to test the answers to these questions has the knock-on effect that it is hard to test methods for improving techniques. Should you practice your nukite in the air, or will that just encourage you to overextend? Is it helpful to practice one thousand a day, or would it be more effective to practice three sets of ten against a pad? Our inability to test our fighting methods restricts our ability to test our training methods.

To be fair, I'm overstating my point a little here. Judoka regularly attempt to throw all sizes of other judoka who are resisting being thrown (though only resisting in certain acceptable ways—you can't poke your opponent in the eye, or pull a knife on them). Sometimes they succeed, and sometimes they don't; but either way, both *uke* (person receiving) and *tori* (person throwing) learn something.

Nevertheless, the fact that so few Karate claims can be straight-forwardly tested, with the results published in peer-reviewed jour-

Say No to animal testing

nals, makes it harder to challenge the beliefs that are held solely out of deference to history or tradition, solely out of a tendency to exaggerate the worth of the things we hold sacred, or solely because we have invested so heavily in them that it hurts to give them up. Just imagine if the situation was as bad in anatomy. That is, imagine a world in which doctors insist that the blood circulates, but forensic anthropologists scoff at the very idea; undertakers swear the heart is in the chest, but physiotherapists insist it is in the *hara*, and sports scientists claim it is an amorphous system spread throughout the core.

No one thinks you can learn true anatomy from a book, and instead you have to train with one of these groups, all of whom will insist that you listen to them lecture whist running intervals and being whacked with a *shinai* by their research assistants. Medical imaging techniques were never developed and it's illegal to cut open a cadaver. Only then would the data poverty in anatomy be as bad as it is in the martial arts.

But the real problem isn't just that we live in data poverty—I think that's true for some perfectly respectable disciplines, including theoretical physics—the problem is that we live in poverty but continue to act as though we live in luxury, as though we can safely afford to believe whatever we're told, as though we don't need to make serious efforts to keep ourselves honest in the face of our own investment and longing for enchantment.

So is my main message that you should scoff at the word of your sensei or senpai? Of course not. That isn't being an epistemically responsible agent either; that's being an asshole. All the old constraints on your behavior still apply. It's important to be *cautious* in what you believe. In the words of the Buddha, copied from their place of honor on the wall of Harry Cook's dojo:

> Do not believe on the strength of traditions even if they have been held in honor for many generations and in many places; do not believe anything because many people speak of it; do not believe on the strength of sages of old times; do not believe that which you have yourselves imagined, thinking that a god has inspired you. Believe nothing which depends only on the authority of your masters or priests. After investigation, believe that which you have yourselves tested and found reasonable, and which is for your good and that of others.

Why It Matters

Why does it matter that the martial arts are rife with epistemic vice? Epistemic vice is not moral vice and a person might combine his gullibility or closed-mindedness with a gentleness or integrity which is morally impressive. Moreover, epistemic vice is *common* and can even be charming. Most of us know intelligent people who have blind spots on certain topics, such as the parent who persists in believing in their child's troubled genius. One recent study even found that men and women who are married often overestimate the degree to which their spouse will be considered attractive by a random panel of judges, and that epistemic error is sort of endearing.

But it would be stupid to believe that epistemic vice is acceptable *in the martial arts*, because this is an area where it is morally important to have true beliefs, and not just cute ones. The question of whether you can stop a train with your *ki*, or whether a stretch will be detrimental to your students' health, or whether a technique could stop or kill someone—these are not questions on which it is acceptable to be endearingly mistaken.

13
Seeing Your Own Shadow

JOHN HAFFNER and JASON VOGEL

Somewhere in a nondescript building near Tel Aviv, a young military officer is taking a Krav Maga class in counter-terrorism. Today he is training for an airplane scenario—he has to learn how to try to subdue a man who is threatening hundreds of civilian passengers with a live hand grenade.

Meanwhile, just outside Shanghai, an elderly woman has commenced her morning Tai Chi routine in a local park before she makes her way to the nearby market, where she makes a living as a vegetable vendor. While the young officer rehearses fast movements to avert terror, the elderly woman is unrushed in her movement, and her mind is at peace.

As the contrast between Tai Chi and Krav Maga illustrates, there can be major differences from one martial art to the next. Beneath the surface, however, there can also be interesting similarities across martial arts. Indeed, in our view, there is at least one theme that is common to all martial arts: whatever else they may be, they can all be seen as an organized form of mental and physical discipline applicable to combat.

Admittedly, in the contrast we just considered, the Israeli officer's training is much more obviously a form of combat than the daily movements of the Chinese vegetable vendor. But Tai Chi can also claim combative roots, and its movements still have practical combative elements. When the elderly woman in Shanghai commences her sword routine, she may not be thinking about ways to defend herself in a dark alley, but the martial heritage to her movement is unmistakable.

To use an analogy from the Austrian philosopher Ludwig Wittgenstein (1889–1951), to say that all martial arts have some relation to combat is to say that martial arts have a *family resemblance* to each other. Individual members of the Smith family, say, may look like one another in some but not all respects. Similarly if one were to assemble a group of martial artists in a room together—whether mixed martial arts competitors or Kali stick-fighting experts—they would exhibit a family resemblance in their shared expressions of combat despite their differences.

With this idea of combat underlying martial arts, like so many branches of a family tree, the question we hope to explore is this: what are the implications of martial arts study for personal development? Does the average person benefit by engaging in a mental and physical discipline rooted in some idea of combat? Do people paradoxically achieve a greater sense of inner peace by practicing combative arts, as is often suggested by practitioners, or do they end up even more violent and angry than when they started? Do martial arts provide a shortcut to wisdom, or do they rather invite self-aggrandizing ideas and forms of self-deception?

Our answer to these questions will be: Yes in all cases. Martial-arts study can open new pathways on one's journey of self-understanding, but beware: it's also full of pitfalls, distractions, and distorting mirrors. Martial arts simultaneously invite self-discovery and self-deception, two themes that have preoccupied philosophers for millennia.

Of Shadows and Light, and Other Opposites

Philosophers enjoy thinking about contrasts and contradictions. Aristotle (384–322 B.C.E.) even formulated *a law of non-contradiction*: he held that a thing cannot both be and not be in the same respect at the same time. This way of thinking runs deep in philosophy: just as a fighter cannot retreat defensively and move forward in attack at the same time, so it is thought that a philosophical argument will hit a wall as soon as it allows a contradiction.

But contradictions, and contrasting ideas, are also quite productive in philosophy. In fact many philosophers who claim to be interested in consistency have actively *sought out* contrasts and contradictions in the belief that they can help their thinking along. Just as some martial artists seek out fights to sharpen their skills, so some philosophers make a point of organizing ideas into clashing principles in the hope that they will be able to gain a more complete understanding of the subject at hand.

The German philosopher Georg Hegel (1770–1831)—who has been called the modern Aristotle—constructed an entire philosophy out of this: not by avoiding contradictions, but by consistently thinking through them, by acknowledging some truth on each side. Let us see then if we can gain a better understanding of both martial arts and philosophy by examining paired opposites, or contrasting philosophical claims, as they arise in the world of martial arts.

Greater Peace or Enhanced Violence?

Look at grainy old photos of martial arts masters, whether Chinese, Japanese, Filipino, or Indonesian, and many of the images will show them seated serenely beside some of their favourite weapons. Which came first: the serenity or the contemplation of violence? It's an odd mix, surely. Yet many martial artists like to say—especially in books they write about themselves—that their study of combative arts has helped instil in themselves a greater sense of inner calm and peace. Books written by martial artists are replete with suggestions that the warrior path is a path to enlightenment, and yet philosophers would surely find this to be an interesting and questionable claim. Why would the study of combative arts, of violent movements and vanquishing opponents, help to instil a sense of peace? Are not violence and peace commonly regarded as opposite states of mind, opposite objects of contemplation?

And yet there is surely something to the paradox, if it is only expressed as a modest idea. Martial artists may find bullies leaving them alone, and may find this fact reassuring. A martial artist may develop greater sensitivity to the threat of violence in a situation before it fully erupts, and so evade it. And through the use of combat skills an artist could save his life, or the life of someone else: reflection on such a happy event may engender in the artist a sense of peace and gratitude.

But martial artists commonly offer a more profound claim: not simply that random movements of violence avoidance can be satisfying for martial artists when they occur, but that the study of martial arts can transform the inner life in enduring ways; the emotional and spiritual center of the artist may change radically for the better. What should we make of this idea?

The answer may depend on what other assumptions we're prepared to make. If we assume that humans are violent and inclined to conflict, it may make sense that martial-arts study could provide a relative sense of calm in the midst of this violence, like a ship with reinforced ballast while buffeted by strong winds on all sides.

Take the English philosopher Thomas Hobbes (1588–1679), who contended that human nature in its natural state was a war of all against all—and so we needed forms of government to protect us from ourselves and each other. Hobbes might have little difficulty accepting that martial arts training can give people a greater sense of peace than if they had no shield from violence at all.

A related idea that could support the 'peace through violence' thesis is that controlled violence allows people to vent negative emotions in a healthy way, lest they are otherwise repressed and later manifest in even darker forms. This idea—that punching a bag can be cathartic—is quite a modern idea, and likely originates with psychologists like Freud, who regarded untamed human nature as a bundle of instincts in need of sublimation and discipline.

On another view, however—a view advanced for instance by Aristotle—character is shaped by habit. Or in the modern version of this idea, motivation follows action. The cultivation of violence through martial arts study may exacerbate the dark and violent side of humanity. Depending on the specifics of their craft, martial artists who engage in visualization exercises may find themselves repeatedly rehearsing ways to inflict significant pain. Still other martial artists, trained to be more aware of their surroundings, may begin to look with more suspicion on other people, amounting almost to paranoia, especially when traveling in public places.

So philosophers like Hobbes might be prepared to see how the study of martial arts instils peace as a shield from an omnipresent war, while Freud might imagine it as a healthy and controlled way of expressing otherwise dangerous or repressed instincts.

But Aristotle—not unlike parents watching their kids play violent video games—might worry about the long-term impact of thinking about violence all the time. It's hard to say what violence lurks in the hearts of others, but in our experience at least some martial artists spend much of their day-to-day life on edge; a mere hair trigger away from a fight. Then again, we have run across martial artists who appear to be in possession of an inner calm, who enjoy a sense of "flow" in their lives, perhaps as a result of their martial arts studies. While we ourselves cannot claim to have achieved peace and enlightenment as a result of martial-arts study, we cannot rule it out for others.

Strength versus Weakness

Parents will recognize variations of this: a young child, after having attended a few months of Tae Kwon Do class as a beginner, begins to see himself as invincible, threatening to kick down the walls of the house or (unfortunately) his unsuspecting younger brother. Among children, especially young children, this idea might seem charming enough.

But the fantasy is not limited to children, and among adult martial artists, such imaginings can take less innocent forms. Many martial artists want very much to believe they are the toughest, the best, the strongest; the one who cannot be defeated. Returning to the law of non-contradiction, however, they cannot all be right all the time: sooner or later almost all of them—even those who prefer to remain big fish in small ponds—will be in for a rude awakening.

For others, however, martial arts study may help to put such fantasies to rest. Especially where the training hall includes realis-

tic scenarios of mortal conflict, martial arts students may become more aware of the huge range of ways in which human beings can be wounded or killed. As a result, they begin to look on their own mortality and health with a greater sense of humility. Indeed, masters of martial arts systems can become acutely aware of violence and danger. Just as we use the paradoxical term "Socratic ignorance" to describe the wisdom of Socrates (470–399 B.C.E.) in knowing so well how little he knew, so some martial arts masters have been left with an enhanced sense of their own weakness and vulnerability after absorbing countless techniques.

In his enduring work of military strategy, *The Art of War*, the ancient Chinese philosopher Sun Tzu (his historical existence is disputed, but scholars place the work in the period 476–221 B.C.E.) underscored the importance not only of knowing the enemy, but also of knowing oneself: "If you know the enemy and know yourself, you need not fear the result of a hundred battles . . . If you know neither the enemy nor yourself, you will succumb in every battle."

The advice of most martial-arts teachers today is even more cautious: there's much to fear in battle, no matter how much knowledge or skill the student may think they have gained relative to their enemy. On any given evening in any major Western city, children and adults participate in mainstream martial-arts classes in which they are admonished not only to study self-defense in earnest, but also to make every effort to avoid violent confrontations. However effective the promise of self-defense training may be as a marketing tool for new students, most martial-arts teachers will acknowledge that the second part of the advice is much more important than the first.

The contrast between strength and weakness also gives rise to another theme of interest to philosophy: relations of power, dominance, and control. Advanced martial artists, through immersion in violence, may become more inclined to bully, control, hurt, or intimidate others. In some cases, these forms of abuse and control can be quite subtle; they may be rationalized as nothing other than the rituals of a dojo, or the manner in which a teacher must correct a student's technique if the student is to improve. The student, meanwhile, who has projected an idea of enlightenment or personal power onto the martial arts instructor, may go a long time before questioning these experiences, if ever—even if they feel subconsciously that something is wrong.

The French philosopher Michel Foucault (1926–1984) was particularly good at identifying relationships of power and discipline in society: for him, the more subtle the power play, the more pervasive it was and the harder it was to get rid of, or change. Even the mere act of observation, he said, can be an expression of power and discipline, and anyone who has felt the gaze of a martial arts teacher, or who has bowed before a sensei, will know what he means. The martial-arts world is full of the use and abuse of these power dynamics: the teacher who insists that a reluctant, inexperienced student must go up against a much more senior student in a sparring match; initiation rituals for belt promotions that look more like hazing rituals than useful forms of training (one of us trained with an organization that blindfolded and then beat candidates for black belt); implicit and explicit pressure on new members to join in competitions to support the gym.

But relations of power are inescapable features of human life. Martial artists are perhaps well served by becoming more aware of them: it makes navigating them simpler, or less destructive. You may become more sensitive to issues of personal power without necessarily abusing this knowledge. In fact the opposite may be true: a martial artist may help empower people who are being bullied or abused, *because* of the knowledge they have gained on this score.

Holism versus Dualism

René Descartes (1596–1650) argued that the core of human nature is the mind and its capacity to doubt and think. The body is a mere extension of the mind—the philosophical equivalent of an afterthought.

This separation of the mind from the body is described in philosophy as 'dualism'. For many philosophers, including us, the separation does not do justice to human life. In contrast to (and in reaction to) Descartes's dualism, other philosophers have argued that human beings are always *embodied*: for human beings, the mind and the body are inextricably connected.

For the most part, martial arts support this idea. Martial artists learn how to work with the mind to improve movements for greater economy, precision and pragmatic effect—or to push their bodies beyond their natural points of reluctance (think of board breaking). They can also learn how to "psych out" opponents through unexpected movements, words spoken, or changes in expression. Martial arts that emphasize competition or self-defense also encourage economy and precision of movement: superfluous movements can be exploited by opponents, and so they're avoided.

The physical sense of play of many martial arts—whether rolling on the ground in Aikido (rolling is something most adults last did as children), or creative kicks in Tae Kwon Do, or acrobatic movements in Kung Fu—all these movements outside everyday motions can help fire new synapses and provide additional oxygen to the brain. These forms of play are ways for humans—as beings *in* bodies—to reaffirm the connections between their mental, emotional, and physical selves (connections downplayed in modern technological society).

Ironically, however, certain forms of martial arts study can also distract from a holistic awareness of oneself: far from overcoming dualism, they reinforce it by suppressing the body at the expense of the mind or vice-versa. This imbalance can occur in martial arts that emphasize extreme training rituals and ascetic bodily practices, where students are encouraged to push well beyond their physical limits. In other cases, the imbalance is on the side of the mind, as in classes that take an overly analytical approach. Improvements for students of *any* martial art require an appropriate balance of sideline coaching and correction, as well as abundant periods of repetitive practice.

If a martial-arts teacher repeatedly interrupts a student from movement practice with editorial comments, and encourages students to be highly analytical and introspective as they move, the teacher is taking an overly intellectual approach to martial-arts study. This problem seems more common in the West, where students and teachers alike are in a broader culture that encourages individual introspection.

Appreciation for or Distortion of Tradition?

What role does tradition play in our lives, in shaping our identities? In the contemporary world, especially in the Western world, it's common to think that we can fashion our identities largely as we like, regardless of culture and language.

But philosophers who think about tradition, like Hans-Georg Gadamer (1900–2002), insist that people can only with difficulty distance themselves from traditions they have inherited and that they should not look on those traditions as necessarily restrictive and stifling of their identities. For Gadamer, tradition is a dynamic concept; not simply something we inherit, but also something we interpret and make our own.

The world of martial arts contains a variety of attitudes towards tradition, both on the part of schools and individual students, and it is not a stretch to say that some of the disputes across martial arts traditions are felt and expressed with the fervor of religion. These spirited disputes are not only interesting in their own right, they also help illuminate the philosophical question of how tradition intersects with identity.

Among Japanese Jiu-Jitsu schools stretching back centuries, for example, there are contemporary factions with rival interpretations and practices, with each side claiming to be the legitimate and true heir of the original art. Modern-day practitioners in these rival schools—even if they live in the United States or Spain—can become quite emotionally invested in their stake in the controversy. Similarly students of mixed martial arts (MMA) competitions nowadays can be dismissive of any art that does not have direct application to their sport, just as students of street survival arts can be disdainful of any art that has been limited as a sport.

While some martial artists may have legitimate reasons for adhering to one particular tradition and dismissing others, in many other cases the attitude is chiefly about dogma or ego—whether of the artist, or the artist's teacher. A martial artist who has embraced one tradition may find it difficult to step back and view that tradition critically, even when circumstances suggest they should do so.

This excessive deference to tradition is a form of self-deception, especially in cases where it issues from a glorified projection onto another culture. It is not uncommon for Western students of Eastern martial arts to ascribe a rational purpose to every aspect of the art they are studying, on the assumption that those rituals have stood the test of time. In some cases, however, those practices began quite recently, or they were first developed for arbitrary, temporary, or local reasons, and only later—through a misleading combination of forgetfulness and reverence across generations—were those practices vested with great meaning.

That's not the only way distortion of tradition can happen: there's also something delusional in the arrogance of a contemporary mixed martial artist who insists that they are not part of any school. Even if they travel from dojo to gym to dojo without claiming allegiance to any teacher, or if they amass techniques from books and magazines, they are still drawing on the traditions of various schools. They still stand on the shoulders of giants, whether they realize it or not.

The Moving Shadow of Truth

There's a widespread myth—especially in the West—that excellence in a martial-arts training hall or competitive ring will also endow the practitioner with other forms of personal excellence: personal maturity, self-awareness, self-discipline, enlightenment, or any of myriad other fortune-cookie virtues.

In some cases, martial-arts study may inculcate some broader personal virtues, such as a sense of peace, a measured awareness of vulnerability, a reminder of the need to honour the body, or a firm yet flexible sense of tradition.

In countless other cases, however, the myth has no correspondence to the reality. The path of martial arts can often be murky and full of shadows that distort not only perceptions of the world, but also perceptions of oneself. A martial artist may believe they're letting go of violence, but through martial-arts study they may embrace more of it. A student may become deluded or drunk on a sense of personal power, and lose good judgment or a sense of ethical boundaries.

Martial arts teachers may believe they are holistic in their approach, only to emphasize the mind at the expense of the body or vice versa. And practitioners may become so attached to an idea of martial arts tradition that they cannot let go of it when they should, or they cannot acknowledge their indebtedness to it when they should.

How can we avoid the pitfalls, the path of shadows and deceits, and instead follow the light of self-awareness and personal development? How easy our task would be if we could find a simple formula for doing this!

As with other philosophical inquiries, however, there is no single path. As we approach what we believe to be the right answer or the right school our circumstances may change—our bodies change, getting stronger or weaker; our teachers emerge in a different light. We can predict with certainty only that we will get older. And as we do, in all likelihood our reasons for studying and practicing martial arts will change as well.

The placid Aikido master, accustomed to teaching harmonious and co-operative movements, may one day need to teach his child how to punch a schoolyard bully on the nose. The professional cage fighter who spent years cultivating an attitude of daring invulnerability may need to learn how to disarm others, to express sensitivity in relating to a spouse or a friend.

The ultimate lesson of martial arts is a lesson dear to philosophy: at times we will see light; at other times, shadows. At times we will need repetitive gym practice or consistent philosophical arguments; at other times, ring conflict and philosophical contradictions will enable us to grow faster. The martial artist matures when they can see the limits of their teacher and make the art their own; similarly Hegel had to uncover ideas beyond the genius of Aristotle and others who came before him. Martial arts remind us that eternal vigilance is needed in the ongoing quest to separate enlightenment from deception as we go about our lives.

14
Budo for Buddhists

CHRIS MORTENSEN

The monk Tripitaka and his disciple Monkey were journeying to the West (India), to bring back the Buddhist scriptures to China. They were set upon by six robbers. The robbers demanded they leave their horse and bag, and depart immediately. Monkey, the guardian, refused and challenged them. They attacked him with their swords and spears, without success. Then Monkey reached into his ear and took out a pin, and waved it in the wind. It magically became an iron rod. He attacked the robbers, who ran away. But Monkey pursued them, captured them, and beat them to death with the rod; then stripped them of their clothes, and seized their valuables.

"That's a terrible thing you have done!" said Tripitaka, "They may have been strong highwaymen, but they would not have been sentenced to death even if they had been caught and tried. If you have such abilities, you should have chased them away. How can you be a monk when you take life without cause? You showed no mercy at all!"

"But Master," said Monkey, "if I hadn't killed them, they would have killed you." Tripitaka said, "As a priest I would rather die than practice violence. Now that you have entered the fold of Buddhism, if you still insist on practicing violence, you are not worthy to be a monk. You're wicked!" Monkey departed in a huff. (From Wu Cheng-en, *The Journey to the West*, Chicago University Press, 1977.)

Can a martial artist, someone who practices *budo*, be a Buddhist? Many martial artists have called themselves Buddhists, of course. What I'm asking about is the extent to which the two are morally compatible. There certainly *seems* to be an incompatibility—as the story of Monkey illustrates. A central precept of Buddhism, part of the Eightfold Way, is *Take No Life*. This has been taken so seriously by many Buddhists that it has been held to justify vegetarianism. But on closer examination, things are not so simple—particularly when the use of martial arts weapons, such as Monkey's rod, are on the agenda. Let's see how.

Take No Life

Let's start with *Take no Life*. The phrase "martial arts" covers a wide range of activities, from the training given to the armies of the world over the centuries, to the activities of your modern Saturday-afternoon samurai who punches the air for recreation. We might agree that killing is required in military conflict, but modern martial artists, in it for the sport, should hardly take life.

But surely even Buddhists should be allowed to defend themselves? Armies can, of course, be used for self-defense. But often they are not. So it would seem wise for a Buddhist not to join a standing army. But what about private self-defense, or defense of one's family, or even of innocent bystanders? There must be a case here.

The Buddhist scholar Peter Harvey tells us that within the Pali canon, the canonical texts of early (Theravada) Buddhism, there is nowhere any justification for violence (*An Introduction to Buddhist Ethics*, Cambridge University Press, 2000; p. 255). He also takes pains to show the great extent to which Buddhists, both Ancient and Modern, have been a force for peace, and for the rejection of violent solutions to political and personal disputes. Modern leaders such as Aung San Suu Kyi and the Dalai Lama, as well as groups such as the Soka Gakkai in Japan, have set fine examples for the rejection of violence and killing.

Of course, killing yourself is killing too. One reason why I was attracted to Buddhism at an early age was the example of those monks who burned themselves as a protest against the obscenity of the Vietnam War. I was hugely impressed by these people who felt such compassion for their fellow humans that they could lay down their lives to save those of others. So is sacrificing one's own life with the aim of helping other people prohibited by Buddhist doctrine? I think not. Stories of self-sacrifice for the benefit of others abound in the Buddhist literature. I cannot believe that it was within the intent of the Buddha to rule out such noble actions.

But what of killing others? Harvey goes on to note various places in the Buddhist literature where certain killings are said to be justified. Some of these places are of Theravadin origin, and others have their origin in Mahayana (the later form of Buddhism). Perhaps the most significant example of the second kind is the *Upaya-kausalya Sutra*. This tells a story which concerns a sea captain who learns that one of the crew intends to kill the other five hundred sailors, and so takes it upon himself to initiate the violence and kill the crew member. The text and many Buddhist commentators take the view that this is the lesser of two evils, and that the captain's intention to save life ensured him a better karmic outcome.

Zen and the Martial Arts

And in practice, as Harvey also notes, Buddhists have not always been so high-minded about killing. Buddhist monks have sometimes taken up arms, for example in defense of their monasteries, which were periodically attacked by local warlords or bandits. In medieval Japan, weapons-carrying monks were known as *yamabushi* (see Oscar Ratti and Adele Westbrook, *Secrets of the Samurai,* Tuttle, 1999). Moreover, Buddhism has certainly been an inspiration to the martial arts in China and Japan. In the case of Japan, Zen Buddhism was an inspiration to the *bushi,* or warrior knights, and their successor caste, the *samurai.* Even as late as the twentieth century, some Zen Buddhist teachers took it upon themselves to provide mental training to military personnel fighting in modern wars.

Buddhism did have an influence on samurai (see D.T. Suzuki, *Zen and Japanese Culture,* Princeton University Press, 1978). But for the samurai, the issue of the morality of killing takes a back seat, for obvious reasons. Indeed, Zen Buddhism is not the sumtotal of the samurai attitude to life: there is some overlap, but neither is the same as the other. Moreover, Zen has a somewhat anti-intellectual flavor, which would have appealed to the samurai, who were, by-and-large, doers rather than thinkers. As Harvey puts it, Zen was appreciated for its "discipline, simplicity and directness" (p. 265).

Zen supplied, as well, a significant doctrine, that of "no mind," *mushin* (see D.T. Suzuki, *The Zen Doctrine of No Mind,* Rider,

1949). This is difficult to describe simply, though it is something of a development of the doctrine commonly seen in both Theravada and Mahayana Buddhism, namely that there is no such thing as a self, that selves separate from the world around us are an illusion, leading to attachments and suffering. In application to martial training, this leads to a certain emptiness of the mind, a watchfulness with no emotional baggage and no hesitation in battle. It produces warriors who are "calm, self-disciplined fighters, with no fear of death" (*Buddhist Ethics*, p. 265).

So we have to be very careful about the implications of Zen and the samurai for *Take No Life*. Still, it would seem that there can be legitimate Buddhist exceptions to the principle. Clearly, though, one should break it only in very extreme circumstances.

No First Strike

What, though, of initiating violence? That looks pretty bad too. Call this principle *No First Strike*. This is a very good rule to live by. It means that any violence that one might participate in would be defensive violence, self-defense. If everyone lived by this rule, then all violence would disappear from the world. It hardly needs arguing that this would reduce suffering, a desirable outcome on Buddhist grounds.

Many notable martial arts masters have subscribed to *No First Strike*. Mr. Funakoshi, the founder of Shotokan *Karatedo*, is famed for saying "In Karate, there is no first strike." He seems to have meant both that one should not start things, but also that Karate training serves one well in fending off a pre-emptive strike. Also, Mr. Ueshiba, *O Sensei*, crafted *Aikido* as a martial discipline intended to be purely defensive.

The martial arts can be broadly divided into two groups, predominantly *empty hand* styles and predominantly *weapon* styles. Among empty hand styles, there are predominately *grappling* styles and predominantly *kick-punch* styles. *Judo* and *Aikido* are examples of grappling styles, while *Karatedo*, *Taekwondo*, and *Kungfu* are kick-punch. These distinctions are somewhat loose: just about all martial arts have elements of all of the above, it is a matter of the predominant emphasis. Still, each of Karate and Judo has something the other lacks. An opponent will usually throw a punch or kick at some stage and it is essential to be able to defend and counter these with Karate; while a judoka can throw, fall, or close inside kicks and punches, go to the ground, lock and strangle.

Karate, Judo, and Aikido can be used to kill, there is no doubt. But it's not so easy, and certainly not as easy as when armed with weapons. So empty-hand styles are closer to the spirit of our first principle, *Take No Life*. What's more, these styles offer excellent defensive techniques, techniques to counter someone else's initiation of violence, techniques in accordance with *No First Strike*. And again, the ability to repel an attack leads to having a certain self-confidence not to begin violence. This explains why, in my experience, trained martial artists are almost always polite and courteous people.

Mr. Ueshiba wanted to create a martial art which avoided death, and even injury, as much as possible. This was Aikido. Watching skilled aikidoka can hardly fail to impress. The attacker's *chi*, unbalanced by the attack, is redirected away from the defender, sending the attacker flying. Training is an exercise in mutual co-operation between attacker and defender: the defender twists the attacker's wrist and the attacker rolls out of it; resistance by the attacker might result in a broken wrist. There is an important point here which speaks in favor of the principle *No First Strike*. That is, anyone who initiates violence unbalances themselves. They seek to leave the space they occupy and invade another's space. But an unbalanced opponent is easier to repel or deflect. In short, the one who begins conflict, other things being equal, is the one who will suffer bad karma from it.

Should *No First Strike* be an inviolable rule, though? Is initiating violence ever a good idea? Well, can't pre-emptive strikes sometimes be justified? There are imaginable military circumstances, I guess, where one might be justified in starting violence: for example, where heavily-armed opposition forces are known for certain to be about to launch an attack which will make retaliation impossible. The usual argument in support is that in such cases the attacker has already inititated the violence, and so such a strike does not violate the principle *No First Strike*. But such arguments applied to the martial arts used for individual self-defense often have an air of artificiality about them, it seems to me—at least if the attacker is unarmed. Worse, they are of the kind that has been used by militarists down through the millennia to justify beginning martial action. One simply has to suspect these motives whenever they are trotted out as an excuse for violence. Hence, it would seem *No*

First Strike is an important principle both for the Buddhist and for the martial artist.

There's one important qualification, however. This is the situation in which you are faced with multiple opponents. Needless to say, any good martial arts teacher ought to be in the business of recommending flight before fight. Against multiple opponents this is even more relevant. Run for your life. Don't believe the dispatch of a dozen nasties beloved by Hollywood and Hong Kong chopsockies. But if flight is unfortunately impossible, then I think that pre-emptive action may well be unavoidable. My old Karate master used to recommend grabbing the nearest weapon and going fast and hard at one side in a flanking movement, with the aim of breaching the lines and escaping. This would give you a better chance then simply waiting for the opposition to make their collective first move.

Stop Before Harm

There is a further important principle about violence with good Buddhist justification, and which the Monkey story illustrates. Not only did Tripitaka criticise Monkey for taking life, he also pointed out that, with such abilities, Monkey should have simply chased the attackers away. Monkey caused gratuitous suffering; and suffering is a very bad thing—for Buddhists especially. So even if we accept the wrongness of taking life and of initiating violence, it must still be asked: how far may one go in self-defense? I like to put the answer in a third slogan: *Stop Before Harm*. This actually has two meanings. First, it can be read as "stop before you do anyone harm". What is the concept of "harm" in this? Examples help: a permanent injury is a harm because it produces suffering, even a broken limb which will eventually heal is attended by suffering and is thus a harm. On the other hand, I certainly don't want to extend the notion so far that *any* thwarting of desires the attacker might have is to count as "harm", particularly if the attacker's desires are to cause harm to me and others. In a similar way, the Hippocratic Oath ("First, Do no Harm") is not seen as a prohibition against, for example, causing unavoidable pain in the interests of affecting the necessary cure. This takes us to the second interpretation of *Stop Before Harm*, namely that it is better to stop an attacker rather than harming them. It may well be possible to stop someone without causing them much harm. I don't think that martial artists always grasp this point, though I am sure that Mr. Ueshiba did.

Weapons and Violence

So we have three general Buddhist principles about violence: *Take No Life*, *No First Strike*, and *Stop Before Harm*. Fine sentiments indeed, but there is an especial complication over the application of these three principles in the matter of weapons. When Monkey got his stick, his fighting powers were much increased. Many martial arts have a component of weapons training, even *Aikido,* that most pacifist of martial arts; and some martial arts specialize in weapons.

Weapons confer considerable superiority over empty hand. A pre-emptive strike with a weapon is more difficult to repel, especially if the defender has only empty hands. In contrast, if the defender has a weapon, then repelling an initial strike is more likely, and especially so if the attacker is empty-handed. That is, proficiency in weapons reinforces the ability to implement the second principle, *No First Strike,* though there is the usual yin-yang trade-off: a person willing to violate the principle will be empowered to do so.

In any case, the Dark Side of this Force is that weapons can kill quickly. The point of the practice of weapons training runs closer to a violation of the principle *Take No Life.* Moreover, the striking power of weapons makes it harder to exercise the restraint required by the third principle *Stop Before Harm*: a blow with a heavy stick, for example, can easily break bones. So, can our three principles be reconciled with the nature of martial arts weapons?

Weapons of Wood

There are very many different kinds of weapons—far too many to catalogue. I will stay with what I know: sticks and swords in the Japanese tradition. This makes for an immediate distinction, between *wooden* weapons and *steel-bladed* weapons. There are notable differences between these weapons in respect of their lethal powers. Wooden weapons are generally less lethal than blades, so wooden weapons represent less threat to our first principle, *Take No Life.* Ratti and Westbrook (*Secrets of the Samurai*, p. 308) record that this found its way into Buddhist practice: wooden weapons such as the staff were frequently preferred among Buddhist priests who wished not to shed the blood of their fellowmen. It's said that the great swordsman Miyamoto Musashi eventually dispensed with the sword in duels, in favour of the wooden bokken. This story is often told with an air of demonstrating Musashi's great superiority. My own explanation is different. Musashi was a man of taste and culture, an artist, and author of *The Book of Five Rings*. The effectiveness of a bokken is little diminished in comparison with the katana, whereas the bokken more readily permits one to win without killing or maiming.

Among wooden weapons, there are the *shinai*, the *jo*, the *bo*, and the *bokken*. The *shinai* is made of several strips of bamboo bound together, with a leather grip and a plastic *tsuba* or guard like that of the katana. In weight it is fairly light, about four hundred grams. This makes it possible to build armor which will protect against shinai blows, which in turn makes possible contact sparring (and brilliantly fast and spectacular international competitions). But only non-contact sparring is practical for the other, heavier, weapons. The jo is a straight oak stick, of variable length around 120 centimeters, and a fair weight of around eight hundred grams. The bo is longer, around 180 centimeters and 1.2 kilo plus in weight. Its weight and length make possible long-distance attacks, such as to the ankle. The bokken is an oaken sword around the size of a katana (100–110 cm) or larger, and weight from approximately eight hundred grams upward.

I stress weight because this is an important factor in weapons. The heavier weapon is generally more destructive. It is harder to block, and can smash a lighter weapon. The heavier the weapon, the easier it is for a blow to kill or maim, and so to contravene all our three principles. However, the lighter weapon has the advantage of being generally faster. So there is a compromise between speed and striking power. The jo makes for a good combination: enough weight to stop a katana but quicker and easier to carry than a longer stick, and its two ends can be used, with appropriate grip changes. In appearance it is just a stick, and so less threatening than more overtly-designed weapons.

Fighting distance, *maiai*, is an important lesson for all martial artists to learn. Empty-hand styles are closer range than weapons, and among empty-hand, grappling is closer range than kick-punch. Weapons of different lengths also differ in their natural fighting distance: the shorter the weapon the closer the range. To illustrate, there is the legend of the invention of the jo. In the seventeenth century, Gennosuke was a young master of the bo. He travelled around to various dojos, challenging the local weapons expert, always winning. Eventually and inevitably, he came to know of Musashi, and so determined to challenge him. But Gennosuke pressed too hard, allowing himself to come too close where he was captured by Musashi's twin swords. Musashi then commented that it was a lesson in fighting distance. Stunned that Musashi had let him live, Gennosuke retreated and meditated on the fight and Musashi's advice. Eventually he came up with the idea for the jo, a compromise weapon, having the reversibility of the bo, longer than a katana and, as we have seen, with good speed and weight. At the second encounter with Musashi, Gennosuke was able to use the length and reversibility of the jo to prevail. In return, he spared Musashi's life. (Two examples of *Take no Life*.)

The Humble Walking Stick

One wooden weapon to take particular note of is the walking stick. Shinai and stick training easily generalizes to the use of walking sticks as weapons. Walking sticks vary considerably in weight, but shinai-weight or heavier is not uncommon. Being wooden, the walking stick has the advantage of being less lethal than a blade. More importantly, against an empty-handed opponent, a walking stick in proficient hands conveys a big advantage. Against a knife, a walking stick can easily deliver the double strike *kote-men* (wrist-head), which is practiced continually by kendoka. How could a knife-person deal with such a strike to the knife-hand immediately followed by a strike to the head? Not well I think; blocks with a knife would not work. Against a much heavier weapon, such as your industry-standard baseball bat (around nine hundred grams), to have a chance one would need a walking stick of comparable weight. Such are not readily available, but it's obviously possible to have them made. Finally, a walking stick has the advantage of a non-aggressive appearance, deriving from its primary use which is non-aggressive. Indeed, the walking stick is the last legal weapon.

Back to the Buddhist Eightfold Way, again. One of its steps is *Right Livelihood*: you shouldn't earn a living from something that harms others—which certainly includes the manufacture and sale of weapons. This poses a problem for the martial artist who wants to train with weapons, in that acquiring weapons for training is collaborating in the bad karma of others. But again there are complexities. Just about *anything* can be used as a weapon. Again, as my old Karate teacher used to say, when faced with multiple opponents, grab the nearest chair, jab and block with it. What matters is the use of the weapon, not its existence. This excuse for harmless practice with dangerous weapons can be pushed too hard. It smacks of the slogan "Guns don't injure people, people do", which is not so convincing. Even so, whatever we say about manufacturing items whose *principal intended use* is as weaponry, walking sticks are okay: their main function is to assist walking!

There's another saying that cemented my attitude to weaponry: *fear a young man's fist, and an old man's stick.* One can have confidence that superiority in stick weapons will last until an advanced age. More, a stick isn't just for men, by any means. A woman proficient in stick weapons can readily defeat a male opponent. This is an important point. It must be conceded that it is difficult for a woman empty-handed to defeat a man, whose weight and striking power are generally much greater. But a woman proficient in

weapons and armed with a stick has a real chance. A woman martial artist friend once objected to me that she could hardly go around armed. Yes, but carrying a walking stick is legal. Moreover, even with heavier sticks, while it might be difficult to make everywhere safe, she can make some places safe: suitably concealed sticks in the house or the car definitely give a protective advantage. And, of course, weapons give either sex a better chance against multiple opponents. So walking sticks are very effective weapons compatible with our three principles!

Weapons of Steel

Steel weapons are a different matter, altogether more deadly than wood. Among blades there is the samurai sword itself, the *katana,* and its shorter version, the *wakizashi.* The katana weighs around a kilo or more. The wakizashi, which was designed for indoor personal protection, is around two-thirds the size and weight of the katana. The katana is not practical as a weapon of self-defense in modern life, if *Take No Life* is to be our governing principle. It's not surprising that wearing a katana was banned by the Meiji restoration in Japan!

Practice with the katana is essentially *Iaido.* Iaido is the art of drawing the sword, cutting one or more opponents, and returning the sword to its sheath (*saya*). Iaido practice with the katana is done with completely focused mindfulness and spirit (*zanshin*). Nothing concentrates the mind so wonderfully as a sharp sword passing within a millimeter of one's fingers. Looking down at the sword as one returns the katana to the saya is seriously uncool, but it doesn't take many lessons to be able to feel the position of the sword with your fingers at the neck of the saya. If you make a mistake, and even the best occasionally make mistakes, it is important that this not disturb your zanshin; just repeat the move.

The katana can be practiced in one spot, or in a more free-flowing fashion which is also called *Kenjutsu.* These contrast two somewhat different traditional applications of the katana (like the six-gun): quick-draw versus battlefield. Quick draw is necessary should violence suddenly erupt, while rapid movement such as in Kendo is inevitable in a battlefield melee. However, sparring with a katana, even a blunt katana, is a not practical, since, apart from the potential injuries, it will damage the weapons, which also explains why sparring with wooden substitutes like the shinai or bokken developed. Many iaidoka choose to learn as a supplement a wooden-stick sparring style such as Kendo or Kenjutsu for this reason.

The katana has a graceful curve, appropriate for a weapon which primarily cuts and secondarily thrusts. I won't hide my fascination. It is, in truth, a beautiful object, even those cheap swords designed only for practice. Drawn with lightning speed, cutting with the moonlight flashing on the blade, elegantly and economically returned to its *saya*, it is poetry in motion. Antique katana, museum grade, are exquisitely decorated. The very best are protected in Japan as National Treasures. The smaller wakizashi is similarly elegant.

The practice of the katana has not always been without moral controversy, connected with our principle *No First Strike*. Ratti and Westbrook (*Secrets of the Samurai*, p. 276) note that quick-draw admits a grey area between defensive reaction and pre-emptive strike in dueling. Of course, dueling is rightly banned, as contravention of *Take No Life*. But there is also the possibility of "treachery" in dueling. In a hair-trigger situation there's room for misperception about who started things. However, some have openly defended a first strike on the grounds that a warrior should be prepared for danger at any time. This is to be deplored, I must say, for it runs quite contrary to *No First Strike*.

What Monkey Should Have Known

So where are we? *Take No Life*, *No First Strike*, and *Stop Before Harm* all have impeccable Buddhist justifications. The principles have to be suitably understood: qualifications are required to deal with self-defense, multiple attackers, attackers with weapons. Weapons themselves generally allow a more effective defense against an initial strike, in line with *No First Strike*. A blade is deadlier than a wooden weapon. This makes wooden weapons preferable for self-defense, if weapons must be used, in line with *Take No Life* and *Stop Before Harm*. A walking stick is particularly to be recommended. This is primarily non-violent, and it can be used by all. It can act as a deterrent, a restraining device, a sharp counter in a wild empty-hand melee, or generally for stamping its authority on a situation before it gets too much out of hand. Monkey, please note.

Monkey image, copyright Heather V. Kreiter/CCP North America/White Wolf Publishing.

15
The Eye of the Beholder

JUDY D. SALTZMAN

I should believe only in a god who understood how to dance.

—FRIEDRICH NIETZSCHE

How can we know the dancer from the dance?

—WILLIAM BUTLER YEATS

Once when sparring during a Shaolin Kenpo class, I executed a defensive side kick, sending my taller, younger opponent crashing to the floor. The technique was accomplished before I thought about it.

Kenpo is not the only martial art in which this happens. An Aikido practitioner once told me that there are times when he "gets into a zone," and is able to throw fast moving opponents, even before he thought about it happening. In the same vein, dancers have explained that they "dance the music, not to the music." After first learning to count bars, and to memorize forms, what they had absorbed became embodied: the dancers became the dance. In the same way, after memorizing blocks, strikes and stances, the fighters become the fight. What's happening here?

The Dao of the Body

In a nutshell, this: the accomplished martial artist senses the Dao (the Way) of the body. Instead of the dualism of the mind instructing the body, the body teaches the mind, and the mind guides the body—they act as one. There's a kind of automatic function, which takes over.

*Judy Saltzman executes a defensive side kick sparring with sensei
Khandi Serpa*

Yet it's more than simple reflex or instinct—there's refinement,
cultivation at work. It only comes naturally after years of work. And
more importantly, it is strikingly, enchantingly beautiful. And this
beauty is somehow enhanced by the thoughtless effort involved.

But why? Why is there such joy and beauty in doing and watching the movement, especially if it is spontaneous and flowing?

This question can be answered by first understanding what is
not aesthetic. When martial arts form is not flowing, and is discon-
nected, choppy, and lacks balance power and precision, it is ugly.
And this is due to some disconnection between the performer and
the form—they've yet to embody the movements and mindset, or
are hampered by ignorance, fatigue, nervousness, or pain.

The beauty comes when there is no separation between the
geometry of the form and the flowing movement of the martial
artist's body. Every serious martial-arts practitioner has experienced
this moment of breakthrough. It's the sudden, freeing flow of the
techniques: a series of discrete movements, combined into a single
moment and mood; the hard, linear punches and kicks alongside
the soft, expanding circles; the combination of the Yang (the hard
and linear) and the Yin (soft and circular) make the form beautiful.

The Birth of Beauty

The German philosopher and poet Friedrich Nietzsche explained this aesthetic in his book *The Birth of Tragedy out of the Spirit of Music*. According to Nietzsche, the aesthetic arises in two modes: The Apollonian—structured, geometric, restrained, and harmonious; and the Dionysian—chaotic, asymmetrical, drunken, cacophonous, and frenzied. Separated, the former is lifeless and the latter is destructive. Unified, they created the art, which became the basis of tragedy, but which also sheds light on martial arts and their aesthetic charm.

For example, in my style, "Shaolin Ch'an Fa" in Chinese or "Kenpo" in Japanese, forms are divided into two general classes: the centerline and the circular. The centerline includes most basic beginning forms, whereas the circular tend to be more complicated, active, and in some cases, longer. This can be illustrated by the most basic form, Mountain Meets River, and its cousin style's Kata 1.

Both these styles of Shaolin Kenpo are based on the geometry of the square, the triangle, the circle, and the hexagon. Both are flowing hard styles, incorporating both the Yin and the Yang. By performing these forms, the Kenpo practitioner merges into the geometry. The otherwise abstract patterns are embodied in the martial artist, and he or she brings the geometry to life.

This isn't simply an abstract or mystical idea. It's grounded in the natural world, and our appreciation of it. The structure of the human body is itself important to beauty. This is because it displays a universal kind of beauty, the Golden Ratio or Divine Proportion: 1:0.618. When a form or a dance is performed, the shape of the body merges with this form. For example, the top of the head to the toe could be 1, whereas from just about three inches below the navel to the toe would be about 0.618. The same proportion exists from the length of the arm from the fingertips to the shoulder, and form the elbow to the fingertips. The same proportion exists in the human head, if it's measured from the crown to the chin, and from ear to ear. Pythagoras and other ancient mathematicians knew of this, and it was taken up by Raphael and other Renaissance painters.

The beauty of the body is a unity of Dionysian passion and pace with these Apollonian forms. Energy and passion thereby become ordered, while structure is given dynamism. As Nietzsche argued, the later idea of the Dionysian meant a *creative deployment* of the passions, rather than just a drunken revelry. Even the Drunken Style, made famous by Jackie Chan, uses this principle. It may appear loose and chaotic, but it takes many years to master. In short, the combination of Dionysian and Apollonian means this: elegant restraint for the first, and fervent movement for the second.

Finding Beauty

What makes a particular form or fight beautiful from the standpoint of the observer? In martial-arts tournaments, criteria for judging a form are balance, power, precision, and intention—acting as if one were in a fight, but combining this with the elegance and confidence of a trained martial artist. The dynamism of the form comes from power and intention (the Dionysian). Without this, the form would be lifeless. The structure comes from balance and precision (Apollonian), without which the form would be chaotic. The two together created a Yin-Yang or soft-hard balance. All of these factors make up the aesthetic value of the form.

But surely beauty is in the eye of the beholder? Can the allure of the form really be *in* the form, or is it simply a matter of taste? Of course judgment may depend on subjective preference. For example, a group of judges in a tournament might prefer the hard, linear geometric Japanese styles, as opposed to the more flowing softer Chinese styles. And this will usually indicate their training.

Nevertheless, there is a common structure in all forms, which is based on an objective aesthetic quality. I agree with philosopher Clive Bell, who said in his essay "Art," in *Reflections on Art* (University of Colorado Press, 1979), "Significant Form is common to all works of art." By this, he meant that any work of art has an internal structure which must be maintained. For example, in a symphony or a painting, even if the style is innovative, there are certain rules such as musical scales and harmony and proportion of figures which must be respectively adhered to, lest the music or art seem inharmonious and clumsy. A good judge will have his or her own taste, but still be able to recognize the "significant form" of a fighter's power, precision, balance, grace.

Living Beauty

But what about martial artists? It's not enough to simply watch. We're not just spectators. How do we *experience* this beauty? To fully understand, we must practice. And after practicing, recognize the moment when our forces—Yin and Yang, structure and drive, linearity and circularity—harmonize. These experiences, although individual and subjective, can be evaluated and shared.

This process begins when we're novices. Often a beginner experiences the excitement of a breakthrough—we suddenly "get it" after long hours of trying. Then there's the further overwhelming delight in doing it well, and having this recognized by your teacher, or by judges in a tournament. There's also the thrill of the simulated combat that sparring creates. For example, I once attempted a left front kick, and then spun to a back kick, only to have it blocked, but then managed to score with a left back counter strike. The unplanned nature of this action made it especially satisfying, since it was spontaneous. And it had the added pleasure of a challenge met and overcome—I rose to the occasion, so to speak. But just as importantly, the development and structure of the combination was alluring. It was beautiful, not simply because I "scored," but because my strike depended on hard work, and the marriage of spontaneity and determined training, linear striking and circular counterstriking. This was a joy I could not simply grasp

Master Bill Mailman instructs sensei Khandi Serpa and the author.

abstractly. I had to *feel* it before I could describe it on paper. It was if energy, form, purpose, and thoughtlessness had united—and it was glorious!

As Nietzsche and Yeats both agree: the ultimate aesthetic happens when the form and the performer, the dancer and the dance, the Apollonian and the Dionysian become one and are dissolved: into pure, mindless movement.

Excalibur

Western Martial Arts

*"Talk is for lovers, Merlin.
I need the sword to be king"*

16
Sir Aristotle and the Code of Chivalry

SCOTT FARRELL

The important thing about [chivalry] is, of course, the double demand it makes on human nature. The knight is a man of blood and iron . . . he is also a demure . . . modest, unobtrusive man.

—C.S. Lewis, "The Necessity of Chivalry"

People get into martial arts for many reasons. Some want to break boards with their bare hands; some want to learn to protect themselves in dark alleys; some want the discipline and focus that results from practicing (and possibly mastering) a competitive, physical sport. For me, getting involved in martial arts was all about wearing chain mail.

If you're scratching your head and wondering what, exactly, chain mail has to do with martial arts (much less philosophy)—well, you're not alone. Let me tell you how I made the connection.

It all started when my high-school history class took a field trip to our local Renaissance Faire. Until that point, I'd considered Western history to be nothing but a tedious list of dates, battles, and kings named "Henry" to be memorized. But at that Renaissance Faire, watching the performers dressed in real armor, jousting and clanging their swords together, I saw history come alive—so close I could actually touch it. When the "knights" let us handle some of their equipment after the show (including their weighty chain mail coats) I knew I wanted to do more than just watch from the audience.

That was nearly thirty years ago, and it was my first taste of the martial arts—Western martial arts, that is. It's a field of martial arts practice that was (compared to the more established and recognized Eastern or Asian martial arts) still very much in its infancy back in the early 1980s. But since then, WMA has grown exponentially as more resources have become available, and more practitioners have become interested in strapping on some chain mail and walloping each other with swords in the serious pursuit of a martial arts tradition stretching back more than five hundred years. In a cover story on the Third Annual Western Martial Arts Workshop in Seattle, *USA Today* listed nineteen national schools and associations currently teaching Western martial arts ("Martial Arts Take a Western turn," March 12th, 2008).

But despite increasing scholarship and interest in the field of WMA, there's still a common perception that martial practices of medieval Europe were artless and crude in comparison to the grace and refinement of their Asian counterparts. Samurai were intelligent and highly trained masters of disciplines like Kendo, Kyudo, and Karatedo; knights were just clanking, unwashed thugs bashing each others brains out with axes and spiky clubs—or so we've been led to believe.

While I was initially drawn to Western martial arts simply by the romantic thought of being a knight in chain mail, I soon began to see there's a lot more to WMA than Hollywood images of clanking sword fights. Recent translations of medieval and Renaissance fighting treatises, such as the *Royal Armouries Manuscript I.33* and the works of Hans Talhoffer and Fiore dei Libri, show that as early as the thirteenth century, the schools of European martial arts were just as encompassing, adaptable, and contentious as those in Asian culture. (More than a few duels in Italy and Germany were undoubtedly sparked by claims reminiscent of "My kung fu is better than your kung fu!")

Similarly, we often think of Asian martial artists as wise and contemplative, while medieval knights are usually portrayed as ignorant and superstitious—often almost willfully so. (Think of the number of historical movies you've seen where some character suggests a scientific or cultural advancement, only to be accused of witchcraft and burned at the stake.)

But just as Asian martial artists followed refined and idealistic codes of military honor, such as the famous Bushido code of the samurai, the knights and men-at-arms who practiced martial arts in Europe had their own code of honorable behavior—called *chevalerie*, or the code of chivalry. As I've come to appreciate the fine points of walloping my friends with a sword (and being walloped by them in return) I've also come to recognize the serious intellectual and moral aspects of chivalry—the code of Western martial arts.

In terms of athletic competition, chivalry is often regarded as nothing but a heightened sense of "fair play." But when talking about a *martial* art, a sporting code that emphasizes "self-control, courtesy, consideration of one's opponent, honor, rejection of deceit, cheerfulness under difficulty and refusal to surrender," as Mark Girouard puts it (*The Return to Camelot: Chivalry and the English Gentleman*, Yale University Press; p. 235), might be thought of as an inherently impractical standard. After all, we're talking about hand-to-hand combat—not a gentlemanly game of cricket. When it's "kill or be killed," you don't worry about things like courtesy or rejection of deceit.

Yet a person of knightly character was (and in Western martial arts, still is) expected to embody character traits that might, at first glance, seem incongruous—even contradictory. In studying the expectations and ideals of chivalry in depth, we find that this contradictory aspect results in a surprising strength of moral values. In fact, looking at the various elements of the code of chivalry in this

way, it's very reminiscent of the system of virtue ethics described by Aristotle in his *Nicomachean Ethics*, where he explores the methods and motives men and women employ in the quest to live a life of virtue.

Let's take a look at the principles of the knightly code and see how this guiding standard of the practice of Western martial arts can help us better understand the ethics of Aristotle—whether or not you have any desire to strap on some chain mail and get walloped with a sword.

The Paradox of Virtue and Chivalry

Any system of honorable behavior derived from a warrior culture is going to place a high value on the principle of bravery—and chivalry is no exception. The exact sort of bravery expected of a medieval knight is summed up in the word *prowess*, which was defined, according to Professor Steven Muhlberger (himself a WMA practitioner), as "a combination of courage and skill at arms . . . and an expectation to undertake dangerous occupations . . . with enthusiasm" (Scott Farrell, "Chivalry Today Podcast #8," <www.ChivalryToday.com/Castle/Podcast/Podcast-Home.html>).

Yet unrestrained violence did not equate with chivalry. In fact, a knight was expected to be gentle, humble, and mild as well as being strong and brave. This sort of dual obligation is embodied in the legendary figure of Sir Lancelot, perhaps the greatest warrior-hero of the Arthurian tales, and a literary figure that many real medieval knights sought to emulate.

In the final lines of *Le Morte D'Arthur*, Thomas Mallory (in the Lamentation of Sir Ector) describes Sir Lancelot, the "head of all Christian knights," in terms of this contradictory aspect: "thou was the meekest man and the gentlest that ever ate in hall among ladies. And thou were the sternest knight to thy mortal foe that ever put spear in the rest" (*Le Morte d'Arthur*, edited by Janet Cowen, Penguin, Volume II, p. 530).

C.S. Lewis, a Christian apologist, war veteran, and himself a scholar of the ideals of chivalry, pointed to this very passage as the perfect example of the elusive but important dual standard of the knightly code. "Let us be quite clear that the ideal is a paradox," he said. "The medieval ideal brought together two things which have no natural tendency to gravitate toward one another. It brought them together for that very reason" ("The Necessity of Chivalry," in *Present Concerns*, Harcourt, Brace, p. 14).

This "bringing together" of two naturally opposed qualities calls to mind Aristotle's writings on virtue ethics. In the Aristotelian outlook, to achieve a state of virtue, a person has to strive to reach a mean between two extremes (*Nicomachean Ethics*, lines 1106a:14–1107b:26). In Aristotle's reasoning, every virtuous quality is bounded by two traits of excess. In this way, Aristotle's approach to virtuous behavior is literally a bringing together of two qualities that have no natural tendency to gravitate toward one another.

Consider Aristotle's discussion of courage, a virtue he considers extremely important. His description is remarkably reminiscent of the chivalric ideal described by Mallory and, later, by Lewis. Aristotle says that courage is the "golden mean," or the perfect balancing point on the scale between two extremes: cowardice and rashness. Being overly meek, Aristotle might say, would make one a coward. On the other hand, being overly fierce—flying into a rage at some minor perceived insult, or charging headlong into a fight without any sort of plan or strategy—marks one as rash or foolhardy (*Nichomachean Ethics*, lines 1115a:6–1116a:14).

Aristotle recognizes that a warrior must possess both meekness and ferocity if he or she is to succeed in martial endeavors. Let either of those qualities go unleashed and you have someone who cannot truly be described as courageous. This is exactly the conclusion that Lewis reaches in his assessment of the qualities of a chivalrous knight: Someone who is "meek in hall" but who can't face the rigors of battle is just as lacking in real courage as someone who is unstoppably ferocious, but can't temper their ferocity with a reasonable degree of restraint or compassion (p. 15).

The Golden Mean and the *n*th Degree

It's easy to not quite get Aristotle's approach to courage (or justice, temperance, or any of the multitude of virtues examined in the *Nicomachean Ethics*), or Lewis's description of chivalry from this perspective. Thinking of courageous or chivalrous character as a sort of half-way point between meekness and ferocity gives the impression of someone who's always balanced, in control, and who never goes to extremes.

As anyone who has studied the martial arts knows, being forever caught halfway between ferocity and meekness does not make you an effective warrior. In the heat of a competitive match, you would certainly expect the combatants to exhibit elevated levels of ferocity. And if confronted by an assailant in a dark alley, martial arts experts would certainly be expected—perhaps even obligated—to abandon any sense of meekness or restraint in order to neutralize the threat and keep themselves safe, as well as protecting any bystanders.

And the contrary is true as well. In training, a martial arts student should be respectfully meek and humble in the company of their teacher or master—any sense of ferocity or hostility will only be an impediment in the learning process. Or, when dealing with young children, for example, a martial artist should be particularly polite and deferential in order to set a worthy example for the youngsters.

In other words, there's a substantial difference between real chivalry and merely clinging to the middle ground between meekness and ferocity. Lewis recognized this when he pondered whether the ideals of chivalry had any relevance in the "modern world." He explained that a person of knightly quality strives to know what blend of these characteristics is required in any situation. The knight "is not a compromise or happy mean between ferocity and meekness; he is fierce to the *n*th and meek to the *n*th" ("The Necessity of Chivalry", p. 13).

Aristotle, too, recognizes that continually striving for a halfway point between two polar attitudes or behaviors (such as ferocity and meekness) doesn't result in moral excellence, but only in eternal mediocrity. Instead, the virtuous person must continually assess and evaluate where, on the scale of virtue, "right action" lies. Once you know the extremities of behavior, the challenge is finding the golden mean that expresses virtue "to the right extent, at the right time, with the right motive, and in the right way" (*Nichomachean Ethics*, lines 1109a:28–29). Aristotle would well understand that meekness "in hall among ladies" is just as much an expression of courage as being ferocious to your foes in battle—both are *right* demonstrations of courageous character, appropriate to the situation at hand.

Jousting for Virtue

Throughout my years of study in the Western martial arts, I've seen a lot of new practitioners strap on their own chain mail and pick

up a sword for the first time. Many of them seem to expect that before long they'll have learned the techniques and reflexes necessary to be sword-fighting masters. (And I'm sure I must have been the same when I first put on a coat of chain mail back in my younger days.) After all, how hard can it be to take up a sword and wallop someone with it?

Unfortunately, what these new students don't notice is the number of fellow practitioners who measure their martial arts experiences in decades, and who, after all that time, are still struggling to learn, to improve, and to master the skills of the art. It's unfortunate because, when these new students realize that engaging in hand-to-hand combat while wearing forty pounts of armor or more and swinging an unwieldy sword isn't as simple and instinctive as it seems to be in the Hollywood epics, they often give up and go looking for another hobby.

The irony here, as anyone involved in any martial art knows, is that they're entirely missing the point (if you'll excuse the pun) of these sword-fighting exercises. The practice of Western martial arts is rewarding not because it comes easily or naturally, but because it is difficult. The same thing can be said for the principles of chivalry and the qualities of virtue ethics.

One of the images we indelibly associate with the Age of Chivalry is the tournament: Armored knights on horseback clashing with sword or lance in order to win a prize and the favor of a fair lady. But customarily, these competitions were more than simply demonstrations of physical skill. The joust was also seen as a test of a knight's character—a forum to develop and exercise moral qualities, including courage, largesse and honesty. (See Maurice Keen's discussion in *Chivalry*, Yale University Press, 1984; p. 99.) A knight who cheated or who failed to show mercy and grace to his defeated opponent was not considered a chivalrous and noble competitor. Martial arts competition was a proving ground for the virtues a knight would need when summoned to real battle.

Lewis recognized this too—in fact, he considered the aim of chivalry to be the creation of this sort of person, who could "deal in blood and iron" when called to fight, but still be restrained, compassionate, and civil in times of peace. He recognized that such an ideal does not come easily, and, in fact, is somewhat contrary to human nature. Chivalry is "something that needs to be achieved, not something that can be relied upon to happen" (p. 16).

Like Lewis, Aristotle knew that virtue is not something that happens naturally. He recognized that a virtue like courage is something that must be consciously nurtured in order to become second nature. Virtue is no different from other technical skills, such as architecture or music (*Nichomachean Ethics*, lines 1103a34–1103b:2)—or, presumably, martial arts—the more you practice, the better you become. It's quite likely that Aristotle would have approved of tournaments as an ideal place to practice both martial arts skills and the ethical virtues of a code of honor. Only after such attitudes become so habitual as to be considered "automatic" does Aristotle believe acting in a virtuous manner—accepting defeat gracefully, or keeping your temper in the middle of competition—will become a source of pleasure in itself.

After thirty years of practicing Western martial arts, I'm still looking forward to the day when *that* happens.

For all his talk about ethics and virtues, Aristotle was supremely practical when it came to admitting the limits of human nature. Despite all our desires to be honorable and ethical, he observed with refreshing frankness, "It is no easy task to be good" (*Nichomachean Ethics*, line 1109a24). Lewis reached a very similar conclusion about the knightly standard of the code of chivalry. For him, timidity or brutality could be chalked up to mere human nature. Chivalry, however, demands more than that. "The (person) who combines both (meekness and ferocity)—the knight—is a work not of nature but of art; of that art which has human beings, instead of canvas or marble, for its medium" (p. 15).

There's no direct philosophical connection between the ideals of medieval knighthood and Aristotle's writings on virtue ethics, but one does provide an intriguing angle of view into the other. It's an important reminder that when we engage in the martial arts—whether originating in East or West, involving katana or broadsword—we're doing more than simply trying to wallop each other. We are simultaneously engaging in moral kung fu; in an ongoing fencing match with our standards of ethics. The martial arts allow us to study the very nature of virtuous behavior by exploring the extremes of our ferocity and our humility as we struggle to find the golden mean of chivalry.

17

The Glove of Wisdom

GORDON MARINO

"**K**now thyself" was the Socratic dictum, but Tyler Durden, the protagonist in the movie *Fight Club,* asks, "How much can you know about yourself if you've never been in a fight?" Although trainers of the bruising art wince at the notion that boxing equals fighting, there can be no doubt that boxing throws you up against yourself in revealing ways. Take a left hook to the body or a trip to the canvas, and you soon find out whether you are the kind of person who will ever get up.

I've been teaching both boxing and philosophy for more than a decade. My academic colleagues have sometimes reacted to my involvement with the sweet science with intellectual jabs and condescension. A few years ago at a philosophy conference, I mentioned that I had to leave early to go back to the campus to work with three of my boxers from the Virginia Military Institute who were competing in the National Collegiate Boxing Association championships. Shocked to learn that there was such a college tournament, one professor scolded, "How can someone committed to developing minds be involved in a sport in which students beat one another's brains out?" I explained that the competitors wore protective headgear and used heavily padded sixteen-ounce gloves in competition as well as in practice, but she was having none of it. "Headgear or not," she replied, "your brain is still getting rattled. Worse yet, you're teaching violence."

Violence on Campus

I countered that if violence is defined as purposefully hurting another person, then I had seen enough of that in the philosophi-

The author and bodyguards

cal arena to last a lifetime. At the university where I did my graduate studies, colloquia were nothing less than academic gunfights in
which the goal was to fire off a question that would sink the lecturer low. I pointed out, "I've even seen philosophers have to
restrain themselves from clapping at a comment that knocked a
speaker off his pins and made him feel stupid." I followed up by
arguing that getting and taking punches makes you feel safer in the
world, and that people who do not feel easily threatened are generally less threatening. She wasn't buying any of it. Then I made
the mistake of making myself an object lesson by noting that I had
boxed for years and still seemed to be able to put my thoughts
together. That earned me a smile and a pat on the wrist.

If I were thrown in the ring today and had to defend the art of
self-defense against the sneering attitude of some academicians, I
would have at least two colleagues in my corner. In *Body and Soul:
Notes of an Apprentice Boxer* (Oxford University Press, 2004) the
MacArthur-award-winning Loïc Wacquant, a sociology professor at
New School University, described the sentimental education that he
received training for three years at a boxing gym in Chicago's South
Side. Professor Wacquant, who earned his red badge of courage by
competing in the famous Chicago Golden Gloves tournament,
insists that boxing clubs are sanctuaries of order, peace, and tran-
quility in a helter-skelter world.

According to Wacquant, whose ring name was "Busy Louie," the gym is *"a school of morality* in Durkheim's sense of the term, that is to say a machinery designed to fabricate the spirit of discipline, group attachment, respect for others as for self, and autonomy of the will that are indispensable to the blossoming of the pugilistic vocation." The machinery often works so well that it forges a kind of mutual affection that is absent from the cool halls of academe. When he left Chicago for a postdoctoral position at Harvard, Wacquant fell into a terrible funk about leaving his fistic family. He writes, "In the intoxication of my immersion, I even thought for a while of aborting my academic career to 'turn pro' and thereby remain with my friends from the gym and its coach, DeeDee Armour, who had become a second father to me."

Carlo Rotella, an associate professor of English and director of American studies at Boston College and the author of *Cut Time: An Education at the Fights* (Houghton Mifflin, 2003), spent a year taking notes in the gym of the former heavyweight champion Larry Holmes. Rotella contends that life is all about hurting and getting hurt, and that there are few courses in life that prepare you for the whirring blades outside your door like boxing. In the introduction to one of the best boxing books ever written, Rotella remarks:

> The deeper you get into the fights, the more you may discover about things that would seem at first blush to have nothing to do with boxing. Lessons in spacing and leverage, or in holding part of oneself in

Philosophizing in the ring

reserve even when hotly engaged, are lessons not only in how one boxer reckons with another but also in how one person reckons with another. The fights teach many such lessons—about virtues and limits of craft, about the need to impart meaning to hard facts by enfolding them in stories and spectacle, about getting hurt and getting old, about distance and intimacy, and especially about education itself: Boxing conducts an endless workshop in the teaching and learning of knowledge with consequences.

Boxing, a School for Virtues

Still, I think the best defense of boxing is Aristotelian. In his *Nichomachean Ethics*, Aristotle offers his famous catalog of the moral virtues. Whenever I teach this section of the *Ethics* I always begin by asking students what they think are the ingredients of moral virtue. Respect, compassion, honesty, justice, and tolerance always fly quickly up onto the board, often followed by creativity and a sense of humor. I usually need to prod to elicit "courage." And so I hector, "How can you be consistently honest or just if you don't have the mettle to take a hit?"

Aristotle writes that developing a moral virtue requires practicing the choices and feelings appropriate to that virtue. Accordingly, colleges today often offer a smorgasbord of workshoplike events to help develop the virtue of tolerance, for example, by making students more comfortable with people from diverse backgrounds. But where are the workshops in courage, a virtue that Nelson Mandela, John McCain, and others have claimed to have found in boxing?

According to Aristotle, courage is a mean between fearlessness and excessive fearfulness. The capacity to tolerate fear is essential to leading a moral life, but it is hard to learn how to keep your moral compass under pressure when you are cosseted from every fear. Boxing gives people practice in being afraid. There are, of course, plenty of brave thugs. Physical courage by no means guarantees the imagination that standing up for a principle might entail. However, in a tight moral spot I would be more inclined to trust someone who has felt like he or she was going under than someone who has experienced danger only vicariously, on the couch watching videos.

In fact, boxing was a popular intercollegiate sport until the early 1960s, when a fatality and problems with semiprofessionals' posing as students counted the sport out. In 1976 college boxing was resurrected as a club sport, and now, under the umbrella of USA Boxing (the governing body for amateur boxing in the United States), the National Collegiate Boxing Association includes about thirty college teams. Every April sectional, regional, and national championships are held. I recently chatted with Maja Cavlovic, a female boxer from Estonia who graduated from the Virginia Military Institute this spring. A power puncher, Ms. Cavlovic reflected, "Boxing helped me learn how to control my emotions. You get in there and you are very afraid, and then all of your training takes over."

The two-time heavyweight champion George Foreman concurs with Ms. Cavlovic. In addition to being an immensely successful businessman, Mr. Foreman directs a large youth club outside of Houston with a vibrant boxing program. Since Mr. Foreman also is a preacher I asked him, "How do you reconcile teaching kids to deliver a knockout blow with Jesus's injunction that we should turn the other cheek?" Mr. Foreman chuckled and explained, "To be successful in the ring you have to get control of your emotions—that includes anger. And the kids who stick with it in the gym are much less violent than when they came in through the door."

Americans for the most part live in a culture of release in which passion and spontaneity are worshipped. Beyond being told that troublesome feelings are medical problems, our young people receive scant instruction in modulating their emotions. As a result, there are very few opportunities to spar with heavyweight emotions such as anger and fear. In the ring, those passions constantly punch at you, but if you keep punching, you learn not to be pummeled by your emotions. Keeping your guard up when you feel like leaping out of the ring can be liberating. After he won his first bout, I asked Karl Pennau, a St. Olaf student whom I trained, what he had gleaned from his study of the sweet science. He replied, "Learning boxing has given me a lot more than just another sport to play. It is a tough, tough game, but having trained and been in the ring, I won't ever think that I can't do something again."

18

Fencing Is the Loneliest Martial Art

NICOLAS MICHAUD

When you thinks of sport, you generally think of a team effort. Similarly, when you think of the martial arts, you rarely think of selfishness and deception. But, words like "selfish" and "deceptive" may best describe the art of fencing. Now, you might say, "Wait a minute; aren't martial arts supposed to be unselfish? Aren't they about growing to understand your opponents better?"

And, yes, although most martial arts are grounded in the desire to protect yourself, many of them have developed into more understanding and compassionate sports. Many martial arts have become sports in which the combatants not only try to defeat each other, but they also try to understand each other—for the sake of greater harmony.

Fencing, though, is solitary; you do not seek to understand your opponent in order to produce a great sense of harmony or well-being; you do not even seek to understand your opponent just to score a touch. You seek to understand your opponent in order to deceive your opponent—and in doing so, win the contest.

When a fencer is "on the strip," he or she is all alone, even when he or she is a member of a team. Perhaps the team seeks a certain number of wins collectively, but this doesn't change the fact that when you're on that fencing strip, you fence alone. Your wins, and your loses, are exactly that—yours. It's difficult to develop a feeling of camaraderie as your success or failure in this particular contest rests solely on your shoulders. There is very little in the way of cheering or raucous noise from the audience; there is no fanfare. There exist only you, your blade, and the enemy.

Jean Béraud's "The Fencer," daring you to be selfish

How Selfish Is Fencing?

For this reason, amongst others, philosophers might consider fencing highly egoistic. More specifically, it echoes the egoism described by the English Enlightenment philosopher, Thomas Hobbes.

There are two kinds of egoism: psychological egoism and normative egoism. Psychological egoism is the idea that people naturally seek their own interests and only their own interests. Normative egoism is the idea that people *should* seek their own interests. The difference between the two is that while psychological egoists believe that we cannot escape from seeking our own interest, the normative egoist thinks that the right thing to do is to seek our own interests.

Hobbes's egoism falls into the psychological egoism category. Hobbes believed that human beings naturally seek whatever is in their own interest. In his book, *Leviathan,* considers what we call the "state of nature." This state is the state in which human beings normally exist without the rules imposed on them by society. According to Hobbes, this state of nature is brutal. As humans have competing interests, those interests conflict and violence is the result. If there's no outside force making us follow rules, we'll all do whatever we have to do to get what we want, regardless of who else may be hurt. To quote Hobbes, when humans are in the state of nature, life is "solitary, poor, nasty, brutish, and short."

A good deal of what Hobbes says makes sense. It does seem that we need someone to enforce the rules in order to make people follow them. Consider a fencing match: there are many consequences for those who don't follow the rules. Breaking a rule can cost a fencer a touch or even result in ejection from the bout. Without these consequences, it may well be that many fencers would ignore the rules if they didn't feel like following them. The evidence to support this claim is the fact that, even with the consequences, athletes still try to cheat. So, it may be that Hobbes is right—we need someone to force us to follow the rules.

Fencing is dissimilar, though, from Hobbes's ideas in at least one important way: fencing might be even more *normatively* egoistic than psychologically egoistic. That is, it actually *encourages* egoism.

One problem for psychological egoism is proving that people *are* only motivated by their own interests. It does seem that we are often motivated by more altruistic reasons. For example, many fencers gladly shake the hands of opponents who defeat them or will concede a touch against them if won fairly.

The psychological egoist will reply that we do these nice things because they benefit us. In other words, you shake your opponents hand not because it is a good or right thing to do, but because it makes you feel good to be an honorable contender.

But this is a dubious argument. How is it selfish to feel good about helping others? Isn't this, really, the very essence of acting unselfishly? So, the psychological egoist's claim is difficult to prove. Although it does seem true that many fencers only follow the rules because they have to, many others may be honorable people, even without consequences.

Perhaps we're not necessarily as selfish as the psychological egoists suppose. But fencing itself is another story. Even if we *are* generous, considerate people most of the time, fencing seems to want us to be egoistic; the sport encourages individuality, solitude, and deception. And, so, it may be normatively egoistic.

Why Fencing Is Egoistic

If it's true that fencing is normatively egoistic, our concern is less with Hobbes's 'state of nature', and more with the rules and goals of fencing itself: what must a fencer do to win? The general idea behind a fencing bout is that there are rules enforced by the director of the bout; as long as those rules are followed, the fencers should do whatever is necessary to win, regardless of honor. (In other words, even if it involves deception.)

Despite the problems of psychological egoism, this may fit rather nicely with Hobbes's ideas. Hobbes argued that there must be an absolute sovereign who enforces the rules. This sovereign or "Leviathan," as Hobbes calls the ruler, is a person, or body of people, who assert their will and ensure that the rules are followed in order to prevent humanity from reverting to the state of nature.

This idea, that the Leviathan prevents the state of nature, neatly describes the development of fencing. Fencing is a very old art. As long as people have been trying to kill each other with sharp, pointy instruments, the development of the martial art of fencing has been a priority. After the development of firearms, fencing duels to the death still took place in order to settle matters of honor. By the sixteenth century, governments eventually began to outlaw these bloody duels. In other words, the state of nature and resulting bloodshed had to be prevented by the governing bodies. Eventually, it was determined that these matters of honor could be settled without bloodshed, and a director was appointed for the bout in order to determine touches without having to use sharp swords. This director is, in essence, Hobbes's Leviathan.

What we have come to understand is that the state of nature, at least in fencing, must be restrained in order to prevent bloodshed.

The 1932 Olympics gold medal match—a barely-civilized state of nature?

Moreover, a supreme ruler must be appointed to enforce that restraint. What is even more interesting is the fact that, in fencing, the state of nature is not wholly a bad thing. The director does not turn the fencing bout into a vigorous hug fest. Instead, the director only maintains certain rules. Outside of that, the fencers are encouraged to be egoistic: they fight alone and do whatever is necessary within the rules to win—hence fencing's normative egoism.

Fencing and Egoistic Deception

This normative egoism goes even deeper than fighting alone and 'by all means necessary'. The fencer is encouraged to do what we would normally consider inappropriate to win; specifically, the fencer is encouraged to deceive the opponent. This is in contrast to some other martial arts and sports, where good sportsmanship and honor require a kind of "honest" competition. Although most sports do rely on deceiving the opponent, the kind of lying which takes place in fencing makes it even more deeply egoistic. Additionally, unlike many other athletic activities, the strongest, fastest, or even the smartest competitor does not win a fencing competition. Instead, the best fencer is the one who can deceive an opponent the most effectively.

This is not to say that fencers do not score touches by being faster. Speed often plays an important role in fencing. Nevertheless, speed alone will not win you the match. Even if your opponent is very fast, simply stepping backwards and blocking your opponent's blade with your own, in what is called a "parry," will prevent your opponent from scoring against you. So, when attacking a more sophisticated opponent you often must cause him to attempt to parry, and while he or she is attempting to parry, you move your own blade around your opponent's blade in order to score the touch. This move is called a "disengage." The disengage is a deception—you make your opponent think you are attacking in one way and then you change the direction of your attack.

Because the disengage is such an effective technique, as fencers, we cannot let our opponents know which parry we prefer to take. If my opponent knows what parry I'm likely to attempt to use to block the blade, my opponent will simply move the blade around my parry and score the touch. For this reason, I must deceive my opponent. I have to make my opponent think that I prefer to take one parry, and, then, at the appropriate moment, take a different one. So, here, we can see two kinds of deception: 1. making your opponent believe that you are attacking one sector when, in fact, you are attacking another and 2. making your opponent believe that you prefer one parry, when in actuality you prefer another.

Should Fencing Be Deceptive?

Now that we can see how deeply egoistic fencing is, we can ask ourselves, "What kind of philosophy rationalizes this deception?" In other words, now that we know that there is a definite push towards egoism in fencing, what argument can we use to explain that fact? Without some argument, fencing might find itself subject to criticism. Normally, psychological egoism can find a defense in the idea that we can prove everyone is really only motivated by their own self-interest. This fact, though, is difficult to prove. Proponents like Ayn Rand, who argue that it is part of our rational nature to pursue our best interest, often defend normative egoism. Moreover, she thinks that most peoples' self-interest is in harmony.

This defense does not do much for fencing. As fencers are not in harmony—one fencer wins and the other fencer loses, we cannot say that Rand's work clearly defends normative egoism in fencing.

We might find some defense for this egoism in fencing in the world of business. Philosophers of business like Milton Friedman and Albert Carr make arguments that might clarify things. Friedman argues in a rather egoistic way that considerations like honor or personal ethics take second place to profit. He believes that if someone, like a CEO, is supposed to be acting for the welfare of the business, that CEO should seek to do things that benefit the company instead of attempting to do what he or she thinks is right. So, if a policy would hurt the environment, but benefit the business, then the CEO should institute the policy.

In this way, we find something of a defense of egoism in fencing; fencers, when in the bout, have no obligation to anyone but themselves. More importantly, as in the case of a business, the primary obligation of the fencer is to win. According to Friedman, a CEO can act unethically when acting for the interests of the company because the CEO's primary obligation is to make money for the stock holders. It might be argued, similarly, that it is appropriate for a fencer to act egoistically because the fencer's primary obligation is to win the bout.

This may not explain, though, why it is okay for the fencer to use so much deception as a means to this end. After all, there are rules that the fencer must follow in order to participate, so why do we allow the fencer to do something that we generally consider to be unethical? Why is it okay for him to be so deeply deceptive?

Albert Carr is helpful here. Carr argues that in business, some deception is permissible because the rules of business are like the rules of a game. In a game, deception is allowed. Simply, deception is part of the rules of the game, so being apparently unethical is okay within the game. Perhaps it is similar for fencing.

Carr does not explain much about why it is okay to be unethical in a game, but one might argue that, because no one really dies by the wins or losses of a game, the normal rules of morality do not apply. In the same way, if no one is really getting hurt in business, then deception is allowed. And, even if someone *does* get hurt, that someone knows the rules of the game and has agreed to play by those rules, so no harm, no foul.

So, then, is that the answer? Fencing is a game and, therefore, anything is allowed as long as everyone agrees it is allowed?

The difficulty here is that fencing is *more* than just a game; it is a martial art. Initially, it could be argued that deception was allowed in fencing because that deception may be the only way to save your life. People used to live and die by fencing. The argument that "all's fair in love and war" seems to apply when my life is at risk. If someone attacks me, and is likely to kill me, many would argue that I am permitted to do anything, regardless of honor, to prevent my attacker from killing me. So, deception is allowed when lives are at stake.

Fencing, though, no longer has such high stakes. We cannot say fencers should be allowed to deceive because lives are at stake. Moreover, we have an even bigger problem: if you remember Carr's argument and our conclusions regarding games, we concluded that it is okay to deceive when *no* lives are at stake. But, then, we have two arguments for when deception is allowed 1. when lives *are* at stake and 2. when lives *aren't* at stake. It seems that one or the other should be true, but not both.

Is Fencing a Dishonorable Art?

This seems baffling at first, but it leads to an important realization. Deception is permissible in some games, not only because lives aren't at stake, but also because all of the participating parties have agreed that lying is permissible, or even desirable. Even if no lives are at stake, a game isn't immoral or dishonorable if everyone agrees to lie.

But this conclusion is too hasty. Doesn't this simply mean the game itself is dishonorable?

In simple terms: yes, fencing is a dishonest, dishonorable game. This is because fencing, as an ancient art of in war, was developed with the soldier's mindset: anything is permissible if it saves one's own life—all's fair in war.

But lives are no longer at stake: fencing has retained its normative egoism, despite changes in society in general, and fencers' lives in particular. They no longer need to fight to survive – but they continue to lie. Moreover, they consciously and happily take up an art that *requires* that they lie.

Perhaps, then, the art of fencing should be discouraged by those who are honorable. If we want more than just winning and self-defense from our martial art, fencing falls short. If we want to become more connected to those around us, and more honorable people, then fencing is not the right path. It offers us a very Hobbesian feast: solitude, egoism, and deception.

19
Why Practice an Unmartial Martial Art?

CHRISTOPHER LAWRENCE

Lieutenant Blouse was standing in the middle of the floor in breeches and shirtsleeves, holding a sabre. Polly was no expert in these matters, but she thought she recognised the stylish, flamboyant pose as the one beginners tend to use just before they're stabbed through the heart by a more experienced fighter.

—TERRY PRATCHETT, *Monstrous Regiment*

When swordfighting is portrayed in movies or on stage, we often see the hero and villain swinging at each other's blades, rather than their bodies. It's rare to see the slightest suggestion the actors are trying to kill each other rather than perform a military ballet.

Yet the chief original purpose of swordfighting wasn't dancing, but violence: to prevent an enemy being able to cause harm, whether through disarming him, disabling him, or killing him.

A duel was a more ritualized form of a swordfight, which imposed certain restrictions on the affair. In most of the European traditions, a formal duel limited a fight to bouts between two individuals, each ready and prepared, using similar weapons and under agreed conditions.

While duels could be settled by death or disablement, they were frequently made more symbolic by the custom of winning by "first blood." The duel was concluded when one participant was wounded, however slightly.

So a victory by first blood places the emphasis more on skill and less on resistance to pain. A determined swordsman would otherwise be quite able to continue despite a light scratch on the torso.

Modern Western fencing is in some ways the descendant of duelling. But it's isolated from its ancestry in two significant ways, due to the nature of the target area, and a convention called "right of attack." I shall explain both swiftly for non-fencers.

There are three swords in mainstream Western fencing, the foil, saber, and épée. All three are used one-handed against a single opponent. But the very stylized forms of the modern weapons make two of the three sword disciplines into forms of callisthenics rather than martial arts. I shall not describe the more esoteric forms of swordplay, such as singlestick and the German Mensur, but much the same comments would apply.

The foil restricts the permissible target to the torso, which is patently unrealistic. The easiest part of an opponent's body to reach is their sword hand, as it is almost always closest to the enemy. The most vulnerable target is the face. But a hit on either of these is regarded as invalid at foil.

The saber is somewhat less fantastical, regarding the target as everything above the waist (based on the historical use of the saber as a cavalry weapon). Yet excluding the legs from being vulnerable makes the aim of the saber fighter to win a game rather than to defeat an enemy.

So neither foil nor saber proposes a realistic target area, which would be the whole body for any martial art designed to simulate realistic fighting conditions.

In addition, both modern foil and saber have a complicated system of rules called "right of attack", determining which fencer's turn it is to hit the other, rather like chess. This is entirely artificial, again pushing both weapons into toys for sport rather than methods of assassination.

The third weapon, the épée, has the closest resemblance to an actual duel. Any part of the body is an acceptable target, and the winner of a point is simply whoever hits first. (Technically there is a requirement that the winning blow has to be scored one-twenty-fifth of a second before the opponent's. This gap is impossible to record with the naked eye, and so is measured electronically.)

So a bout at épée still bears a considerable resemblance to a duel to first blood, albeit with a vastly lower risk of serious injury.

Why does it matter how similar to the original form of duelling is the modern sport? Do we lose or gain anything of importance by substituting an elaborate game for formalized murder (apart from the obvious advantages of there being fewer dead people)?

And secondly, what is the purpose of practicing a martial art where the risks and stakes are deliberately lowered?

Someone might reply that all martial arts are somewhat ritualized, and many have some limitation on the action. Boxing, for instance, has the Queensbury rules, which restrict the legal target to above the waist, and limit the forms of the attack to using the hand, and then restrict the hand further to permit only punches rather than slaps or scratches.

There is some callisthenic value to any martial art—any form of exercise has some advantage over sloth. However, two points can be made in reply to this approach. First, in the case of fencing, its health benefits are slight. Fencers invariably tend to develop in a one-sided and unbalanced way: right-handers will exercise their right forearm and left upper leg far more than their counterpart limbs. (Technically, this could be avoided by fencing with each arm on alternate days, but I've never met anyone who does this seriously.) Such one-sided development badly hampers the fencer's abilities at other sports.

What We Get from Fencing

And more subtly, it would be nice to reveal the *distinctive* benefits of fencing—a combination of virtues lacking in more common exercises. Many martial arts can claim they give the practitioner some skill at self-defense in an emergency, but this is barely true of fencing. Time spent at the épée may well improve reflexes, co-ordination, and confidence. But virtually *any* other martial art would help you more in a night-club brawl (with the possible exception of Aikido).

So if not working out or self-defense, what else do we gain from fencing? There's a certain courtesy in the sport: you salute your opponent, the presiding judge, and the audience before a bout and you shake hands with your opponent afterwards. This might make the game more agreeable, or give you a reason to encourage your children to take up the épée, but still seems a secondary consideration. It makes the pursuit of fencing a more civilized pastime than less gentlemanly hobbies, but the etiquette is for the fencing, not the fencing for the etiquette.

So what else is distinctive about the épée? We have agreed it is a relatively safe way of imitating an antiquated weapon. But why practice an unmartial martial art?

The Author, Looking Unprepared for a Brawl

I have three suggestions. The first is that fencing is very unusual amongst martial arts: the qualities you need to excel are strikingly different from other fighting disciplines.

First, you need have virtually no ability whatsoever to endure pain. (In my own case, this is just as well.) Most forms of fighting require some ability to take punches or kicks as well as give them, and yet to carry on with as little impairment as possible.

Second, the amount of physical strength you need is much slighter than at, say, Boxing or Judo. Parrying an attack properly is usually best done by moving your point noticeably, your hand slightly, and your shoulder barely at all. (This is the exact opposite of the way fencing is usually portrayed in stage or film fighting, where actors too often show effort rather than effectiveness.) A hand movement of a couple of inches is often enough to block a lunge, while your opponent has to move forward several feet. As it stands, virtually no healthy individual can lunge five feet forward in the time it takes another such fencer to move his hand two inches. So, while speed and reach are important, technique and timing are vastly more so.

What's critical for a good parry is reading your opponent, timing your own defense correctly, and understanding the angles at which the sword blocks or controls another sword.

So we have a game which values psychology, timing, and dexterity over physical strength, stamina, and endurance. So you might expect fencing to appeal to people with the first set of qualities.

Why some of us value the first set of qualities over the second is a question for another time. I personally find Odysseus a more attractive hero than Ajax, as the former generally conquered enemies by guile rather than brute strength. But why I have this preference may well be more a question for a psychologist than a philosopher.

One response I've met with from Dr. Damon Young is that a preference for outwitting your enemy by dexterity and guile does have a touch of aristocratic, officer-class mentality about it, whereas superior physical strength and endurance is more what you want in your porter. This explanation has *some* plausibility in Anglophone countries with the remains of an aristocratic system, where fencing is chiefly performed in military regiments or prestigious schools and universities. But we'd need another kind of story for countries where fencing is much more widespread culturally, like France, Italy, and much of Eastern Europe.

The second strand of my explanation is that sword fighting has appeal as part of a historical tradition.

Sir Richard Burton famously took the view that "the history of the sword is the history of mankind." Such a claim may seem far-fetched, but swords in one form or another have indeed been used in thousands of military encounters between the Bronze Age and the end of the Victorian era.

There is, to me at least, a certain appeal in feeling that I am participating in the same kind of activity that people have been enjoying for well over four thousand years. And depending on your preferences, perhaps a story could be told either of progress—to a modern sport—or regression from lost chivalry.

Swords Have Names

But what I'm most curious about is a third idea, which may explain the sword's distinctive appeal compared to other forms of fighting. The sword has a romantic attraction which goes well beyond its actual effectiveness in combat. Obviously, modern firearms have an unfair advantage on any weapon before gunpowder, but there is a line of thought that quarterstaffs would be more effective against an unarmored man. Their vastly greater reach would more than compensate for the sharp-pointed deadliness of a sword.

But swords make an appearance not only in history, but in a vast amount of literature. And it's striking that an astonishing number of these swords are given names: Arthur's *Excalibur*, Lancelot's *Arondight*, Siegfried's *Nothung*, Beowulf's *Hrunting* and *Naegling*, Bilbo's *Sting*, and Roland's *Durendal*, are almost as well known to lovers of the epic as the names of the heroes themselves.

The tendency to name swords is much more recent than the invention of weapons. Homeric heroes didn't personify their weapons in the same way.

This tendency to give names to objects is true of very few other weapons I can think of in Western literature. Daggers, quarterstaffs, axes, and so on simply don't seem to have an identity of their own, separate from whoever is using them at the time. Still less do guns.

To what other non-humans do we give names? Horses, certainly, and domestic animals in general, but it is easy to recognize that animals have distinct personalities. What inanimate objects qualify? Ships are the strongest contenders, and are almost always given female names in Western cultures. Other forms of transport often qualify, from space shuttles to trains. And the occasional weapon, like the First World War gun Big Bertha.

This leads to the idea that there is something about a sword which makes it more than merely a tool for completing a task. Instead, the elegant, precise nuance of the sword suggests it has a character of its own. It possesses a sense of personality, with its own quirks and eccentricities. Certainly the vocabulary fencers use suggests this kind of emotional connection. A skilled fencer has the '*sentiment du fer*', the feeling for the blade, the emotional understanding of the weapon. And a bout between two able fencers is often referred to as a 'conversation with the blades'.

The Personality of the Épée

What kind of personality does an épée bout have, or by emotional extension, an épée? Swordfighting has at least five qualities which are distinctive, though not unique.

First, facing someone at close quarters with a melee weapon requires an element of courage, which a distance weapon doesn't. It puts your body at risk, however great the difference between you and your opponent. But this closeness is shared by any non-gunpowder weapon, or hand to hand fighting.

Second, there seems to me an element of honor in using a sword, which has cultural overtones of duelling and the idea of a fair fight, rather than, say, a knife, which to my mind has associations of darkness and assassination. It's true that certain Mediterranean cultures like, say, eighteenth-century Spain, sometimes fought duels with knives, but the general idea holds: swords suggest honor, knives may allow it but incline against.

Third, swords have a degree of deadliness compared to non-edged weapons. While you could kill someone with blunt weapons, or even unarmed, I imagine that would tend to be a much less efficient, lengthier, and messier process.

Fourth, there's a definite aesthetic appeal to a sword over weapons like a mace or a club: possibly connected with a Platonic appeal to its fitness for a unique purpose. Swords are designed solely for combat, whereas knives, or staves, or flails are adapted for it from less bloody pursuits. They seem to fit, with admirable precision, their martial aims.

Fifth, sword combat gives a degree of intimacy to the participants which is hard to describe using the tools of logic, but is part of a fuller understanding of philosophy—it explores the subtle emotions which make us human. This emotional link in combat can be felt and recognized by anyone who's enjoyed the distinctive relationship you have with anyone with whom you've fought a memorable bout. A.E. Housman puts this well:

I did not lose my heart in summer's even,
    When roses to the moonrise burst apart:
When plumes were under heel and lead was flying,
    In blood and smoke and flame I lost my heart.

I lost it to a soldier and a foeman,
    A chap that did not kill me, but he tried;
That took the saber straight and took it striking
    And laughed and kissed his hand to me and died.

(*Collected Poems of A.E. Housman*, Wordsworth Edition, 1995, pp. 144–45)

Possibly many kinds of physical combat give the same kind of intimacy. But we have three elements which are distinctive of fencing compared to other forms of physical combat: it requires unusual physical and mental qualities for a martial art, which make it more akin to chess in valuing psychological guile over physical force.

Next, swordplay has a long historical tradition which it is a pleasure to be part of: few twenty-first century sports have been performed continually, in one form or another, since the Bronze Age.

And finally, sword fighting is not only a game, an art, and a martial discipline, but also has a distinctive personality of its own, expressing or encouraging qualities like courage, precision, honor, aesthetic beauty, and the ability to understand someone else's psyche. However little these excellences may describe the actual fencer, there are worse personalities to aspire to.

20

What Makes Fencing Unique?

JEREMY MOSS

It's often said that the reason people are fascinated by dueling and fencing is not because they offer the possibility of killing, but because of the thrill of confronting death and living to tell the tale. People are drawn to fencing in films and novels, and to the fencing piste itself, because there is something fascinating about squaring off against an opponent, weapon in hand. Facing death with a casual disregard is one of the romantic images we have of fencing. Part of the reason for the hold fencing has on the popular imagination stems from its swashbuckling image. From *The Three Musketeers* to *Pirates of the Caribbean*, fencing has been cast as a romantic if somewhat bloodthirsty pursuit.

But fencing is also a martial art, with a rich tradition of debate and scholarship. Beginning in the early sixteenth century, fencing masters produced texts about fencing technique, often lambasting their rivals for their "school tricks and juggling gambols," as English Fencing master George Silver put it (quoted by Richard Cohen, in *By the Sword*, Pan Macmillan, 2003, p. 33).

Yet, apart from the practical concerns about being able to defend oneself, dueling has often aroused fierce moral debates. Philosophers, in particular those who were also fencers themselves, have had a charged relationship with dueling and fencing. Rousseau and Schopenhauer found dueling ridiculous and the physical requirements of fencing laughable. But the moral debate about fencing centered on whether people should be allowed to kill each other outside of state or church jurisdiction. For most of the last five centuries this view had nothing to do with a concern for the well-being of the combatants. Kings, Popes, and Prime

A French fencing school, 1628 (note the "juggling gambols")

Ministers were more concerned that their "human resources" were being wasted. Nor was the concern to outlaw dueling in particular connected to any kind of pacifism. The notoriously warlike Pope Julius II issued a papal bull against duels, perhaps not wishing to share the Church's right to punish.

Defending Your Honor

One of the reasons that dueling and fencing survived numerous attempts to outlaw them was because of its perceived role in defending a person's honor. Philosophers have, in the past, commented on how important this aspect of dueling was. Immanuel Kant thought that a distinction should be made between killing someone in a duel, which was only manslaughter, and murder. Likewise, Jeremy Bentham proposed that dueling be given the same protection as defending oneself against attacks on the person. For both philosophers the honor that was preserved via dueling was a social and personal good.

Giving a good account of oneself in a duel, and in later ages in the more formalized sport, was also a feature that some considered unique about fencing. Behaving fairly, respecting opponents even in defeat, was seen as an expression of good character. In the duel's high age, how a person conducted themselves while fencing was often as important as any technique. Richard Burton, one of Britain's most famous explorers and translator of the *Arabian Nights*, liked to think fencing gave an insight into national character claiming that "how people choose to defend themselves is as much part of national character as literature, costumes, or cooking" (*By the Sword*, p. 21). While this might be the case, it's no more true of fencing than of any other martial art.

Nor are we likely to find our answer to the question of what's unique about fencing by looking at the psychology of fencing. As the duel's accomplice and direct descendant, fencing—even modern Olympic fencing—gains some of its attributes from its imitation of the psychology of combat. One of the things that attracts people to fencing is the skill required to "work out" your opponent and breach his or her defense. There's also the thrill of engaging in simulated combat, especially in a competition. But, essential as these features are to the experience of fencing, they are most likely shared by other combat-based sports. Kendo will have many of the same features, for instance.

That modern fencing still has romantic appeal probably derives from its connection with dueling. But really the connection is hard to maintain. People don't fence to preserve their honor anymore. Nonetheless, some might claim that behaving in an honorable way is still part of the uniqueness of fencing. In one sense this is true. Fencing bouts cannot be started until a salute to your opponent has been given. Moreover, this must be done with the mask up. Sledging, and other similar behavior, are not really in the spirit of fencing, and the rules of modern fencing also allow for a range of penalties for poor conduct. But this is probably not unique to fencing as other martial arts also have elaborate rules of etiquette. In addition, as a modern international sport, fencing is no more or less prey to all the ills that intense competition can bring, and has its share of cheating, drug taking, and other problems.

Fencing's associations and popularity vary from era to era, but its uniqueness is hard to pinpoint. There's something unique about Fencing, and philosophers can, if nothing else, come up with a definition of what that thing is. Fencing is best separated from its dueling past, as there are particular things about the modern practice of the sport that make it unique.

Fencing, or at least foil fencing which I will discuss here, shares several things in common with other martial arts. First, martial arts are often associated with a particular "way of life" which can be better or worse than other ways of life. Fencing certainly has *some* principles it adheres to, though it is rarely associated with the larger conceptions about the world and how to live in it. Second, like other martial arts, it has its origins in combat and preparing for combat. It took off as a sport as the possibilities for using swords in combat decreased. Third, it shares with weapons sports, like Kendo, the excitement of facing someone else in a contest while holding a weapon. Fourth is etiquette, which is supposed to be polite and respectful both to opponents and referees, though without the elaborate reverence that is often associated with martial arts. In each of these cases, fencing has some kinship with at least *one* other martial art.

Distance Makes the Difference

So it isn't the contest, its origins in combat, or its physical nature that make it a unique sporting practice. All these characteristics are true of boxing or Karate as much as they are of fencing. The fact that there is a weapon involved does make it different to many martial arts but obviously not to some, like Kendo.

But the weapon does make for one crucial difference, which offers a clear distinction from many other sports. First of all, the weapon helps to set the distance between two fencers. What this means is that two fencers will typically stand further apart during a bout than, say, two boxers. Whereas boxers will have to never be much more than a quick step and an arm's length from one another, fencers will usually be at least the length of their combined blades plus their arm length away from each other. If a fencer steps in too close to his or her opponent, he runs the risk of being hit while he is preparing his attack. Beginner fencers are taught the importance of "keeping distance" with their opponent.

The distance that is part of a fencing bout allows for a complexity of action and movement that is one of the unique features of the sport. Because of the distance between two fencers, they cannot usually just reach out and hit one another. A fencer will have to move into range to hit an opponent and the time it takes to cover the distance between two fencers allows for a complex combination of movements and strategies. These would not be possible if there were a shorter distance between the two combatants. Elaborate feints with one's blade, false starts, quick attacks and luring your opponent with an inviting unprotected target area all form part of fencing "phrases." Phrases are built up from separate actions; attack, parry riposte and so on; one of the reasons, no doubt, why the sport is often called a kind of physical chess. For instance, one of the simplest but most effective strategies is to move toward one's opponent for an attack to their middle torso, draw a parry, but then disengage one's blade and hit them on, say, the shoulder. All this happens while moving forward and adjusting your distance in line with your opponent's movements. The combination of distance and weapon is part of what differentiates fencing from other martial arts.

What also enables a greater freedom of movement is the very small possibility of being seriously hurt. If you ever walk into a fencing club and look at two fencers on the piste, one thing that will be immediately obvious is that they are well protected. Mask, jacket, breeches, under plastron, even lightly padded socks mean that bruising and strained muscles are the worst injury a fencer is likely to suffer. This may not seem like an important feature, but it makes a huge difference to both the psychological experience of fencing and to the range and intensity of movements that are allowed.

This is added to by the lightness of the weapon, which can be held and moved just with the fingers and thumb. For a start, being able to hit your opponent without fear of hurting them or being hurt yourself frees a fencer to hit with intensity and a huge range of movements. There are so many ways to combine the distance between two fencers and what they do with their blades. A fencer does not have to worry about how vulnerable a particular attack will make her, except insofar as she might lose a point. This invulnerability is also psychologically liberating because it gives a fencer license to attack without any of the moral guilt that such an attack would attract if physical harm were a possibility. And this is surely part of what attracts many to the sport. Having actual physical contact makes for a more restricted sport.

A further feature that makes fencing different is the concept of "right of way", which is easiest to explain by describing a bout. Two fencers start a bout by facing each other either side of the middle of the piste. Once the bout has begun points are awarded for hitting your opponent on their target area, which is basically the torso covered by a metal lamé attached to an electronic scoring device. But points are not awarded just for hitting your opponent or even for hitting them first. To get a point a fencer must have right of way, that is, to have started their attack first or by taking right of way from their opponent by touching his or her blade. This feature of fencing is very much removed from the martial origins of the sport, where all that matters is that you hit your opponent before they can hit you. But when combined with the distance requirement, it adds a further layer to the complexity of the possible fencing phrases.

Back to Square One

Another feature which is not quite unique but certainly not widely shared with other sports, is what we might call the "neutral possession" requirement after a point is scored. In many sports, after scoring there will be some advantage given to one of the teams or competitors. In soccer, the team had a goal scored against them will kick the ball back into play from the center. Similarly, in basketball one side will start with the ball. But fencing requires both fencers to go back to a neutral starting point after each point. Coincidently, Australian Rules Football is one of the few other sports to have this feature, along with Karate and Tae Kwon Do "point" fighting competitions.

The timing, distance, invulnerability and right of way together make for what is unique about the sport of fencing. Its origins may lie in training for real combat, but the modern sport has features that its ancestor does not. I am not claiming that each of these features is unique; individually they are all shared with other sports. But their combination in one martial art is what is different about fencing.

What's unique isn't necessarily what's attractive. The appeal of fencing no doubt does have a lot to do with its history. This is certainly true in the popular imagination where it has a certain romance. But what is unique about fencing relates to the rules and regulations of the modern sport. For all its romanticism, the moral code it might embody and its combative nature, fencing's uniqueness comes from this: its unique rules, the distance they create between two fencers and the protection that allows a freedom to compose and execute movements. Modern fencing is thus able to offer a unique refinement of a very old martial tradition.

And in the Blue Corner, Wearing the White Pants

SCOTT BEATTIE is a legal geographer, and he isn't quite sure what it means either. He also works as a Teaching and Learning Co-ordinator at Victoria Law School. Scott's books include *Community, Space, and Online Censorship: Regulating Pornotopia* (2009) and *Connect + Converge: Australian Media and Communications Law* (with Elizabeth Beal, 2007). Starting in Karate, he has since moved on to Wing Chun, which is more suited to his relaxed disposition.

SASHA COOPER runs Felicifia, a utilitarianism webforum, and gets kicked a lot (no connection, as far as he knows). Over the years he's graded in about forty martial arts, though seldom above the level of white. Having trained in Judo for several years, he was delighted to find that he could effectively counter all throws by lying on the ground, hugging anyone who came within reach, and calling it 'Brazilian Jujitsu'. He now stands up only when someone's offering to punch him.

SCOTT FARRELL has been strapping on chain mail and being walloped by his friends for nearly thirty years, which has given him a particularly personal view of the virtues of chivalry (especially "humility"). He met his wife, April, while practicing Western martial arts, and the two have been swinging swords at each other ever since, resulting in some confusion (and worried phone calls) among the neighbors. Scott explores the philosophy of chivalry through his Chivalry Today Educational Program <www.ChivalryToday.com> and happily points out that while King Arthur may have founded the Round Table, he never had his own podcast!

BRONWYN FINNIGAN is amazed that she still hasn't been struck by *keisaku* while debating monks at Kodaiji Zen temple in Kyoto. When she isn't facing *keisaku*, she works towards a PhD in Philosophy at the University of Auckland. She specializes in ethics and philosophy of action, and also works on Buddhist Philosophy.

JACK FULLER runs a research program called "Politics and the Brain" (not an oxymoron) at the think tank Per Capita. He studied neuroscience at the University of Melbourne, where he contributed in a very small way to understanding the sting ray spine, pain in rats, and schizophrenia in humans. His early mishaps in Karate were offset by the minor glory of the Queensland History Teachers Association prize for an essay on Roman 'hippies' (Epicureans). But he now believes our age needs Stoicism. And more push-ups.

JOHN HAFFNER is a Canadian in his late thirties, who has been reading philosophy and studying martial arts since his teenage years. Earning frequent flyer points the hard way, John has been punched, kicked, and strangled by legendary martial artists in Brazil, Canada, Thailand, and Japan. He has also competed in BJJ, Judo, kickboxing, Seikendo, and Shooto. In philosophy, his high water mark was reading—and for a time thinking that he understood—Hegel's *Phenomenology of Spirit*. The lead author of *Japan's Open Future: An Agenda for Global Citizenship* (2009), John is pursuing several environmental projects in China.

TAMARA KOHN once practiced martial arts as an escape from academic stress, but then she had a cunning plan: to make Aikido communities a new 'field' of research. Training trips overseas became 'work'! Her latest edited book demonstrates this in its title: *The Discipline of Leisure* (2007). After years of training and teaching in anthropology and Aikido in the US and UK, she moved to Australia. A senior lecturer at Melbourne University (School of Philosophy, Anthropology, and Social Inquiry), Tammy lives with her son, dog, an array of swords, and the virtual Other (who doesn't pay board).

Before studying philosophy, **KEVIN KREIN** led a simple and happy existence skiing and climbing in Alaska's mountains. This all changed when he became a graduate student. Within months of starting work in an academic department, he began to feel urges to hit people and things. Rather than unleashing aggression on fellow scholars, Kevin began studying with Sensei Burt Konzak at the Toronto Academy of Karate. Eighteen years later, in addition to teaching Karate classes, he is an associate professor of philosophy and outdoor studies. He returns to his simple life as a climbing and skiing guide in the academic off-seasons.

CHRISTOPHER LAWRENCE is a professional playwright, who still occasionally dabbles as a philosopher. He earned his doctorate from Oxford University, where he thoroughly enjoyed reading

Schopenhauer and Nietzsche with his students for five years but was irked by the utter triviality of much contemporary academic nonsense which masquerades as philosophy. To keep up a rapidly fading appearance of dashing debonairness, he likes to fence every other day. Christopher has fenced in eleven countries so far, finding it most agreeable when meeting new people to stab them as quickly as possible.

When **JOSEPH LYNCH** is not getting beat up, he's a professor of philosophy at California Polytechnic State University. With his few remaining brain cells, he does work primarily in philosophy of mind and philosophy of religion. His interest in the martial arts led him to found the Society for the Study of Philosophy and the Martial Arts. To prove that he is really nonviolent and peace-loving, he also edits "Between the Species," an online journal focusing on animal ethics.

Where **GORDON MARINO** grew up, it was important to learn how to duck. There were always fists and backhands flying. After an amateur Boxing career, Gordon went pro but had an incompatible manager. He tried to quit his contract. When this failed, he, like many pugilists, went back to Kierkegaard. Gordon took his doctorate from the Committee on Social Thought, and unemployment predictably welcomed him. But a position came up at the Virginia Military Institute, where Gordon was soon Boxing coach and professor of philosophy. Gordon continues to train amateurs, and is the Boxing writer for the *Wall Street Journal*.

NICOLAS MICHAUD teaches philosophy at the University of North Florida and Florida Community College, Jacksonville. When he began Fencing he came to realize that duels to the death are a far more effective means of solving philosophical problems than argument. He can now be found running up and down the University halls with his Fencing foil yelling "en garde!" and "tally ho!" To be honest, he looks rather silly.

CHRIS MORTENSEN was born in Rockhampton, Queensland, and studied at the University of Queensland, where he majored in philosophy and mathematics. He spent most of his career at the University of Adelaide, eventually becoming Hughes Professor of Philosophy. He retired in 2005, and now works on a project aimed at describing mathematically the so-called impossible images of Escher and others. He has had a life-long interest in Buddhism, and has trained in the martial arts for thirty years, including Karatedo, Kungfu, and budo weapons.

JEREMY MOSS specializes in political philosophy, with a particular interest in equality. Sadly, his Fencing opponents do not believe in equality. As Director of the Social Justice Initiative at the University of Melbourne, he also has research interests in climate change, welfare, and health inequalities.

PATRICIA PETERSEN is a Karate black-belt, philosopher, author and playwright. In her spare time she's a political candidate. (She's as likely to be elected as she is to wear a pink Barbie *gi* with tassels.) In true Karate style, she never stops trying, failing, swearing, and trying again. As a young child, she learnt Judo. It took her over two decades to realize that her first grading—from Tenth Kyu to Fifth Kyu—wasn't actually a demotion. This grievous wound, like many others, is healing slowly.

GRAHAM PRIEST lives in Melbourne, where he practices Shitoryu Karatedo. He is Boyce Gibson Professor of Philosophy at the University of Melbourne. He is also a Professor at the University of St Andrews. When there, he trains at a Shotakan dojo, and endeavors to contort his body into Shotokan shapes. He is an Australian National kumite referee and kata judge. But just to prove his lack of judgment, he writes books on logic and metaphysics. For fun, he also writes papers on Buddhist philosophy. He loves opera, and is convinced that Verdi wrote a now lost opera about Karate.

GILLIAN RUSSELL has a PhD in philosophy from Princeton and a black belt in Karate from TKRI. She suspects that her dad is more impressed by the latter. She teaches both philosophy and Karate at Washington University in St Louis, and has also trained in Judo, Aikido and Shinto Muso Ryu. Her sincere, careful study of the martial arts has given her a deep appreciation for ibuprofen. She'd like to thank Amos Danielli, Chris Teter, Bill Bridenbaugh, and Anais's guinea pig, Larry, for agreeing to appear in the photos that appear in her chapter. No guinea pigs were harmed in the making of her article.

JUDY D. SALTZMAN has an MA in philosophy and a PhD in religious studies. She is a Professor Emeritus in philosophy at Cal Poly, San Luis Obispo. She spent twenty-nine years trying to teach the young to examine their lives. (Glutton for punishment in other words). She started studying Shaolin Kenpo at the age of fifty-eight, and found it a good way to manage grief after her husband's death. She now holds black belts in two different styles of Kenpo. She loves to do forms, to hit the punching bag, and to participate in "old bag sparring."

RICHARD SCHUBERT is Professor of Philosophy at Cosumnes River College, Sacramento, and Hapkido Instructor at the University of California at Davis Experimental College. He spends his time at Cosumnes fantasizing about improving his Philosophy students' academic performance by dropping classes into pushup position for inattention. He spends his time at UC Davis fantasizing about fostering relaxation in his Hapkido students by subjecting them to the academic lectures his Philosophy students sleep through.

KOJI TANAKA started doing Kendo at the age of six and retired at the age of eighteen. At the height of his career, he was third *dan* (third-level black-belt). In his retirement, he enjoys being a philosopher at the University of Auckland. He mainly works on logic but also works on Buddhist Philosophy as well as Chinese Philosophy.

TRAVIS TAYLOR is a well versed 'pub philosopher' who has been struggling with both martial arts and ethics since pushing around, and being pushed around by, other kids in the sand pit. While trained as an Art Conservator (publishing the exciting sounding 'Database of Oriental Papermaking Fibres'), he has also spent a fair bit of time getting the snot beaten out of him in the name of self-improvement. He initially trained in various arts before finding that Judo offered a great combination of take-offs and landings and has been gaining frequent flyer points ever since.

JASON VOGEL is a Canadian musician in his late thirties who studied traditional Japanese Jujutsu for more than twenty years and taught professionally for ten years. Grasping after fame, money, women, and power, he also studied a wide variety of other martial arts, including Escrima under the blind sword master Nanoy Gallano, and Chinese martial arts under legendary Wushu master Pan Qing Fu (made famous by the movie *Iron and Silk*). Jason has a Master's degree from Le Grande Ecole de Vie. He pays the bills helping people buy and sell homes in Toronto, Canada (Jason@jasonvogel.ca).

DAMON YOUNG is an Australian philosopher and author, with bone-shattering Karate kicks (his own bones, sadly). Damon's black belt in Gojuryu Karatedo didn't intimidate critics of his first book, *Distraction* (2008). His short time in Judo was very 'instructive', which is a euphemism for 'protrusion of the C3/4 vertebrae'. An Honorary Fellow of Philosophy at the University of Melbourne, Damon has written for newspapers, literary magazines, and academic journals. But he still finds Aikido bewildering. More on Damon: <www.damonyoung .com.au>.

The University of
Hard Knocks

SCOTT BEATTIE: Being of a scientific bent, I never really took the idea of pressure points and *chi* meridians all that seriously, until I was temporarily blinded during *kumite* by an accidental pressure point strike. Luckily, a steady diet of Jin Yong novels and Hong Kong exploitation cinema reassured me that nothing in my head was broken otherwise I would have been pretty freaked out. Now I live in constant fear of the mythical 'bowel release' point.

SASHA COOPER: Twisted and occasionally broken pride, but otherwise disappointingly few serious injuries. Also bloody nose, bloody nose, bloody nose, spam, bloody nose, bloody nose, bloody nose, and bloody nose.

SCOTT FARRELL: Two fractured ankles (doing martial arts while wearing fifty pounds of gear is not easy on the joints); a cracked rib (received, unfortunately, just a few weeks before I was scheduled to play the role of King Arthur in a stage production of *Camelot*—and trying to sing with a broken rib is a true test of fortitude and endurance); more groin shots than I care to count, including one that resulted in a trip to Urgent Care . . . and "My friend hit me with a sword," is not the sort of answer an on-call resident expects to hear to the question, "How did you injure your testicle?", and enough random bumps, scrapes, and bruises that when we recently purchased a new refrigerator, we had to get the one with the largest ice-maker capacity in order to ensure we'd have enough ice on hand for the ice packs we (my wife and I) use when we come home from practice every week.

JACK FULLER: At school lunch-breaks we played a sparring game balanced on a beam: the aim was to fight the other person off without falling off. My friend had just begun Judo; I had started Karate, and as far as we were concerned, we were the titans (except I was very skinny). 'Fighting' was defined broadly—the only rule was not to pull your enemy off the beam as you fell. Fortunately, we needed no impartial judge: I took such a big 'run up' I fell off the play equipment and broke my arm. I knew that success in Karate required concentration. But it took me a while to learn what exactly to concentrate on.

JOHN HAFFNER: Broken finger (Judo opponent turned away quickly; pin inserted to heal bone); broken nose (from a punch)—I needed to use women's foundation to conceal the bruising under both eyes when I attended a business conference a few days later in Tokyo.

TAMARA KOHN: Dislocating shoulder is my specialty served up with a string of expletives that makes the bravest sensei wince. I can usually put it back in myself, but I haven't had the same luck with fingers— the little things just won't pop back without medical assistance, so now, alas, they are ugly, and my life's ambition is crushed (Tammy the Famous Hand Model). Black eyes. . . . I seemed to get one at almost every summer and winter camp for a few years. A senior Japanese sensei once saw me in a martial-arts supply shop in California and stared at me for a while before lighting up and saying "*Oh* it's *you.* Why no black eye?!" Often I'd start my university lecturing in the warm autumn with bruises up my arms and a spectacular shiner—the women in the front row always looked particularly distressed on my behalf (I'd laugh and say: 'If you think this is bad, you should see the other guy!').

KEVIN KREIN: There was the broken rib from walking into a front kick during my black belt test. As well, there is the knuckle that flattened when I punched that board that didn't break . . . of course I had to hit it again even as my hand was swelling . . . the board broke when I hit it a third time . . . as of yet, the knuckle has shown no signs of reappearing. How did I break my fifth metatarsal? I am pretty sure I tripped over myself while sparring. And oh yes, I seem to have a bruise that doesn't really go away, instead it just grows and shrinks and migrates up and down my arms and legs. Whenever I think it may have completely healed, I just have to look a bit harder till I find where it has moved.

CHRISTOPHER LAWRENCE has never been injured in twenty-five years of fencing. Unlike many other martial artists, fencers do not regard how much they bleed as a source of pride.

JOSEPH LYNCH: In my first week in training in Kempo at the Pit my left floating rib was broken. A week later, my instructor broke the right rib. He pointed out that he had avoided the injured left rib at least, and maybe now I'd learn to keep my elbows in. A senior instructor broke my nose to begin the sparring portion of my greenbelt test and then complained that I had bled all over his new white *gi* (I believe I wrote about this in the article). I served as a "justice of the peace" for a day and performed the wedding for one of my philosophy colleagues with a black eye earned in my brown belt test. I thought the shiner was barely noticeable but photographic evidence shows otherwise. Finally, I had a bad concussion, or so they tell me. I never went down and my instructor commented it was my best sparring to date. I couldn't remember having sparred at all. So, I immediately went for medical attention, and then had to lecture for four hours straight in philosophy of religion classes. As far as I know, I never drooled or passed out during lecture, or at least no more than usual.

GORDON MARINO must have a flexible snoot, as he's one of the few boxers he knows who has not had his nose busted. However, the day he signed on as pro, he came home with two black eyes. His mother took one look at him and started weeping. He was surprised at her reaction, because he knew she had a reputation as a street fighter when she was a teenager, and *she* would have clobbered him if he ever let anyone push him around.

NICOLAS MICHAUD believes Fencing is quite safe. Despite this, he once tragically lost a toenail.

CHRIS MORTENSEN: Due to an over-optimistic estimation of my ability to execute a jumping turning kick at over forty years of age, I tore a cartilage in my right knee. I endured intermittent restrictions of movement for several years. Fortunately I found a martial art where training was possible with that injury, Kendo. Eventually I sought arthroscopic surgery. Medical science is a wonderful thing! I was back in the dojo in nine days. My only restriction is that I can't sit in seiza. But I ask you: how much of a loss is that, do you really yearn to sit in seiza?

JEREMY MOSS: experience in health inequality could not stop him suffering a nasty sub-coracoid impingement (shoulder).

PATRICIA PETERSEN: Concussion (saw stars a couple of times); broken nose (looked like a football forward on three occasions); my jaw is still a bit out of alignment—was broken a few years ago; blocked a kick to the head—broke my ulna (arm); learnt to make a proper fist after dislocating two and breaking one finger (er . . . not a fast learner it seems . . .): was determined to win a competition at any cost - cracked five ribs; was reminded of the importance of pulling back toes when front kicking after I dislocated my middle toe; with no opponent in sight, stupidly broke my toe on the mat—at this moment, realized my greatest enemy was myself.

GRAHAM PRIEST: broken thumb; dislocated fingers (three occasions)—and probably a few toes too; black eyes (a couple); cracked ribs; once, about an hour after training, my elbow just seized up (fluid on the joint); the usual collection of bruises, pulled muscles, and so on; bruised ego (far too often).

GILLIAN RUSSELL prides herself on being the least injured senior member of TKRI, but has to confess that she hasn't gone entirely unscathed. She would particularly like to thank her training partners for the current shape of her nose, and Fruit of the Loom for the permanent weird bend in her right ring finger. Next time she's kneeing someone repeatedly in the head she'll remember to pay more attention to what she's wrapped her hands in.

JUDY D. SALTZMAN has taken a few lumps. She sprained her ankle after being footswept during sparring. She was also knocked cold after a roundhouse punch from a much younger and bigger male opponent. (When she woke up, she still wanted to fight more.) Aside from various bruises from blocking and punching, she still likes the applied aspect of Kenpo: play fighting.

RICK SCHUBERT: Hapkido emphasizes movement from one's center. After two dozen shoulder dislocations and five fractured metatarsals I realized: my movement should involve connection *to* my limbs, not separation from them. I *might* remember the concussions flattening my learning curve—but my memory's not so good. I do recall that my Taekwondo training was immediately effective; punching trees until the blood ran down not only made my knuckles harder but also buttoning my jeans. Of course, it was Aikido weapons that taught me *ukemi*, the art of blending. My phalanges and metacarpals finally blended together as did my third and fourth cervical vertebrae. It seems "*ukemi*" can also be translated "Move or enjoy the arthritis!"

TRAVIS TAYLOR: Bloody noses, bruises, and a body temporarily twisted into various pretzel-like shapes have been my reward for training. While never seriously hurt, I tap faster than a team of Irish dancers; I have spent a fair bit of time staring at the ceiling of my dojo after getting buried in the mats.

DAMON YOUNG: "Do you want ice-cream with those crushed nuts?" asked my Karate sensei, my groin throbbing. Amazing what a well-timed kick can do to a man's dignity. Also hilarious was the split lip from a five-on-one brawl (try drinking from a straw with a hole in your cheek); the blood nose (you should've seen the other guy—he was fine); the fractured tarsal bones (proof that Thai kicks are better); and the black eye (perhaps I did it myself). But the apex of my clumsiness was the protruded cervical disc from Judo. Judo: it's especially 'gentle' when you're passed out!

Fighting Index

PREPARED BY DAVID SWEENEY